C O O K B O O K

Mark Ellman and
Barbara Santos

with Sergio Perez and
Jose "Pepe" Vega

PENDULUM PUBLISHING
2003

Library of Congress Catalog Card Number: 2003097487
ISBN: 0-9652243-3-3

Barbara Santos
Pendulum Publishing
291 McLeod Street
Livermore, CA 94550
(800) 805-8300

Mark Ellman
Maui Tacos Corporate Offices
834 Front Street, Suite 102
Lahaina, HI 96761
(808) 667-9390
eatmaui@maui.net
Maui Tacos Products: www.MauiTacosCookbook.com
Restaurant info: www.MauiTacos.com

Cover layout and design: Linda Davis at Star Type, Berkeley
Cover photos: Tony Novak-Clifford
Additional photos: Roger Kea

Printed in the United States

First printing: 2003

MAHALO

We want to thank so many people.
So, we decided to do it
the Hawaiian way—with a Mahalo Page.

Mahalo from Mark:

Maui Tacos could not be what it is without the people that make it work every day. Without them we would not be. Mahalo to Maui Tacos Executive Chef Sergio Perez and Director Jose "Pepe" Vega who have been instrumental in making sure we get better everyday.

A special thanks to Cindy Beadles, friend and office manager, who swam the rough waters every inch of the way with me.

I want to thank Shep Gordon—friend, mentor and partner.

I want to especially thank my three daughters, Tina, Ariana and Michelle for living with a madman . . . and my wife Judy for the brains, love and support behind the madman.

And, finally, mahalo to Barbara Santos, friend and writer, who made sure this book was written and published.

Mahalo from Barbara:

A heartfelt "thank you" to Mark and Judy Ellman, John Tullius, Sue Dyer and Bruce Wiggs. They all give nothing but support, 100% of the time.

A big kiss to my equally supportive husband Richard. He helped tremendously with this book and has been my partner for three decades.

Thanks kids—Liz, Dane, James, Cheryl and Abigail, and my granddaughter Allyssa, for loving my cooking (most of the time) and me (unconditionally). Mahalo to Anne (my mom) and Karen (my sweet sister) who taught me to appreciate the power of food on so many levels.

And, finally, Terrie Eliker and Linda Davis for artistically and patiently birthing this cookbook with us.

And to all the people of Hawaii . . . especially of Maui,
Mahalo from both of us!

TABLE OF CONTENTS

THE MAUI TACOS STORY

*One day a successful restaurant owner looked out to the ocean from the
lanai of his Lahaina beachfront home. In silence, except for the persistent
crash of the waves, he brought a glass of mango iced tea to his lips.
He contemplated life, death, the surfers waiting for the next wave . . .
and how it all related to food. This was something he did a lot,
being a celebrity chef and all.*

*To the world it appeared he had everything. He owned a trendy restaurant
on Front Street. His life was filled with visiting movie stars and recording
artist friends. Almost effortlessly, he won culinary awards and loyal
devotees for his island-inspired Pacific Rim cuisine.*

*Oh, outwardly he loved the Maui lifestyle. But damn it, he was craving
something. As the sun set into the Pacific with a neon green flash, he realized
what was missing. Deep inside he had an overwhelming desire for the
simple Mexican food he grew up eating in Los Angeles.
What would he do?*

Chef Mark Ellman introduced his concept of Maui-Mex food at the first
Maui Tacos restaurant in Napili in 1993. It didn't take long for the local "coconut wireless" to spread the word. The first rumblings were with the
surfers. "Hey dude, the food is awesome!"

While Mark adored Southern California's version of Mexican food, he
developed the new Maui-Mex recipes partly because the traditional ingredients weren't readily available on Maui . . . not even tortillas. No worries!
Chef Mark had food supplier connections and there were lots of Hawaii-
grown ingredients that ultimately added a deliciously fresh flavor to his
Maui-Mex recipes. He vowed to use healthy cooking techniques, too.

Mark and Judy Ellman

Looking back, it was logical to combine the Mexican and Hawaiian cuisines. Both incorporate lots of rice, luscious tropical fruit, and fresh-caught fish. Marinated meats and chicken are grilled or roasted outdoors to bring out extra flavor. Fiery-hot chiles provide spice in Mexico and chili water is used by the locals in Hawaii.

Think about it . . . Hawaiians enjoy foods from around the world and that has always made Hawaii a fun place to eat. Whether their ancestors arrived by outrigger canoe from ancient Polynesia or on a jet from Hollywood, the good folks of Hawaii would never abandon the foods they loved back home. When Maui-Mex blended the "best of two worlds", it made perfect sense.

***In went the pineapple; out went the lard. Soon the Maui-Mex
way of eating evolved into a full-blown food phenomenon.***

You'll love the simplicity of Maui-Mex food. It's no-fuss, economical and full of flavor. This isn't snooty, get-dressed-up-to-dine kind of food. As Mark says, "It's Mexican food with Mauitude!"
This cookbook can make your life an endless, tropical vacation. Well, okay, we are pretty sure the recipes in this book will remind you of Hawaii or your favorite Maui Tacos restaurant.

Enjoy a "Surf Burrito" today. Then go outside and applaud the sunset . . . or bike up a volcano if there is one nearby. You might even flash a "shaka" greeting to your next-door neighbor.

**Stop by for a recharge of ALOHA at a Maui Tacos if you can . . .
and always "Live Life with Mauitude."**

MAUI TACOS FAQS

What's up with that name . . . Maui Tacos? There are more **BURRITOS** *than* **TACOS** *on the Maui Tacos menu.*

We truly love our burritos and tacos equally. "Maui Tacos" just looked better on the sign.

What if I can't find an ingredient called for in a recipe?

Substitute, experiment, and have fun with your food. We do! Try a new kind of cheese, chop up some red peppers for extra flavor or go crazy with yellow tomatoes in your burrito. You always get extra credit with us for raising the nutrition value of a recipe. Try using spinach leaves or shredded cabbage when a recipe calls for lettuce.

I'm hungry now. I don't have time to set up a barbecue and grill the meat. What can I do?

It's okay to use leftover chicken or steak from last night's dinner. In fact, next time you fire up the grill, plan to cook up extra and even different kinds of meat and chicken. You don't need to trek out into a snowy backyard, either. Use a ridged cast iron or Teflon coated "grill pan" right on the stove for cooking marinated meat.

Why do the Maui Tacos restaurants have a "surf-shack" theme?

Surfers are the original—and still the best—customers of Maui Tacos in Hawaii. These super athletes get intensely hungry and demand tasty meals that are portable and inexpensive. That used to mean a "plate lunch" in a Styrofoam box. It wasn't the healthiest way to eat but, hey, surfers do get a lot of exercise . . .

Maui Tacos changed all that. We offered a fresh cooked meal wrapped in a tortilla. The surfers loved it. The Maui Tacos menu still offers food you can enjoy at the beach. Even if you can't take a drive along Honoapiilani Highway when the waves are pounding or check out Ho'okipa with its legendary monster waves, Maui Tacos aims to make surfers feel at home anywhere from Kihei to Atlanta!

How can I find out more about Maui Tacos?

Go to the website at www.MauiTacos.com.

MAUI-MEX BASICS

Sometimes—if you are lucky—an awesome south swell
keeps you at the beach and out of the kitchen.
Sometimes it's just a long day at work.
We know you are a busy person . . . but try to make your own
Maui-Mex basics. Why? It's the most reliable way to
duplicate your favorite foods served at Maui Tacos.
Need a better reason? You will be in control of the
seasonings, fat and salt content of your food.
That's an important part of our "healthy eating" philosophy.

BEANS

RICE AND POTATOES

TORTILLA CHIPS

MAUI-MEX MARINADES
AND MEATY FILLINGS

MARK'S TRADITIONAL PINTO BEANS

Pinto beans are served as either a separate side dish or incorporated into recipes. Mark's recipe is so simple, fast and easy . . . you may never reach for canned beans again.

2 cups	dried whole **pinto beans**
1 cup	**onion**, chopped fine
1	**bay leaf**
2 teaspoons	**salt**
2 teaspoons	granulated **garlic**
8 cups	cold **water**

Thoroughly rinse the beans under cold water removing all dirt, pebbles and rocks. Add all ingredients in a large stock pot. Bring to boil and then to a steady simmer for 1½ hours or until tender. The liquid will reduce during the cooking and should just cover the beans when done. Cover the pot only if the liquid evaporates too quickly.

To store: Cool, then store beans in their liquid in the refrigerator.

Makes 4 cups of beans (in a savory liquid)

SIMPLY SMASHED
REFRIED BEANS

No, refried beans don't have to come out of a can.
This recipe uses the entire batch of cooked pinto beans
in the recipe above . . . more than enough for 4 large burritos.

¹/₂ cup	vegetable **oil** (optional)
4 cups	cooked **pinto beans**, drained
	(use recipe on previous page 3)
	salt to taste

Heat the vegetable oil to 300 degrees in a heavy bottom frying pan (or use a non-stick pan). Add the pinto beans. Heat thoroughly but do not let the beans burn. Using a potato masher mash the beans in the oil until coarsely mashed. Add salt to taste.

Makes 4 cups of beans

MAUI TACOS BLACK BEANS

*These beans are excellent as a side dish or in recipes. Forget the overnight
soaking routine . . . Mark's recipe makes a batch of tender beans in record time.
Mmmmm, smell those beans simmering . . .*

2 cups	dried **black beans** (or turtle beans)
1 cup	**onion** (chopped fine)
1 tablespoon	**salt**
2 teaspoons	granulated **garlic**
1	**bay leaf**
8 cups	cold **water**

Wash the beans under cold water thoroughly until the water runs clear. Make sure
that any pebbles or rocks are removed.

Place all ingredients in a large heavy bottom sauce pan or a stock pot. Bring everything to a boil . . . then turn down to a low simmer. Cook for $1^1/_2$ hours or until beans
are tender but not mushy.

The only way you can screw this recipe up is to let the beans burn. Check fre-
quently to be sure the water level stays above the beans during the cooking process.
However, the liquid should just barely cover the beans when the beans are done.

To store: Cool the beans in the liquid and store them (still in the liquid) in the refrigerator.

Makes 4 cups of beans (in a savory liquid)

PEPE'S REFRIED BEANS DE JALISCO

Chef Pepe's secret? He sautés an ancho chile, then mashes the cooked beans in the same pan. It gives his refried beans a sweet smoky flavor that is irresistible.

2 cups	**dried pinto beans**
7 cups	**water**
1/4	**yellow onion**, chopped
2 cloves	fresh **garlic**
2 teaspoons	**salt**
3 tablespoons	**olive oil**
1/2	dried **ancho chile**

Place beans, water, onion, garlic and salt in a large saucepan with a heavy bottom.

Bring to a boil. Reduce heat to medium-low and cover the pan. Always keep the beans covered with water. Cook for 2 hours . . . or until the beans are very tender. Pour off excess cooking liquid, but reserve it for mashing the beans.

During the last 1/2 hour of cooking the beans, soak the dry chile ancho in a shallow bowl of water until the chile is soft.

In a different pan, heat the olive oil. Add the chile ancho and sauté for a minute.

Add the cooked beans and just a bit of the cooking water to the pan. Use the back of a large wooden spoon to thoroughly mash the beans. (If the beans seem dry, add just a bit of the cooking liquid until they have a creamy consistency.)

Stir the beans and chile together in the pan until they are completely blended.

Beans can be kept in the refrigerator for 3 or 4 days.

Serves 4 to 6

SERGIO'S DRUNKEN BEANS

(Frijoles Borrachos)

Chef Sergio says these beans are representative of the area around Monterrey, Mexico . . . one of the first regions to enjoy beer. Since the alcohol is cooked out of the finished beans, you won't get drunk on these drunken frijoles.

Beans:		
	1½ pounds	dried **beans**
	3 to 3½ quarts	**water**
	1	large **onion**, halved
	6 cloves	**garlic**, peeled
	1 tablespoon	**lard** or vegetable oil
Sauce:	½ cup	**lard** or vegetable oil
	1	large **onion**, finely chopped
	3	large **tomatoes**, finely chopped
	4	serrano or jalapeño **chiles**, finely chopped
	1½ cups	**cilantro**, finely chopped
	2 cups	**beer**, light or dark
		salt to taste

Beans: Clean and rinse the beans thoroughly. Soak overnight in water to cover. Discard this water before proceeding.

Combine beans with onion, garlic and lard in either a large heavy pot or a pressure cooker.

- If using a regular pot, add plenty of water (about twice as much water as beans) and cook over low heat for 1½ to 2 hours. Add more water if it evaporates during cooking.

- If using a pressure cooker, add enough water to cover the beans. Cover and cook for 45 minutes to an hour. Cook the beans until they are tender with either method. Drain the beans, but leave a bit of cooking liquid.

Meanwhile, prepare the sauce: Heat lard in a heavy frying pan. Add onion and fry until lightly browned. Add tomatoes, chiles and cilantro. Add the cooked beans and beer. Salt to taste.

Continue to cook over low heat for about 45 minutes until the mixture thickens.

To serve: Pour the hot beans into a large clay or individual ceramic serving dishes. Serve the beans with roasted meat and warm corn or flour tortillas.

Makes 8 servings

MAUI-MEX RICE

... just the way they do it at Maui Tacos

This technique may be ambitious for the home kitchen. But if you want the authentic flavor of Maui Tacos style rice . . . go for it!

1 cup	long grain **white rice**
2 cups	**vegetable oil**
¹/₂	**onion**, chopped fine
1 teaspoon	**salt**
1 teaspoon	granulated **garlic** (or 1 clove minced)
3 cups	vegetable, chicken or beef **stock**
1 tablespoon	**tomato paste**

Place the rice in a metal mesh strainer. Heat oil to 350 degrees in a pan large enough to hold the strainer and immerse the rice in the hot oil. Fry the raw rice in the oil for one minute or until it turns white. This will par cook the rice so it cooks faster. It also toasts the rice for a nice nutty flavor.

Bring the other ingredients to a boil in a heavy pot. Add the fried rice. Reduce heat, cover and simmer for twenty minutes. Let sit for ten minutes and then serve.

Makes 2 cups

MAUI-MEX RICE

. . . the home version

This is a one-pan version of Maui-Mex rice. Easier to make, but still using all the same ingredients they would use in the restaurant.

1 cup	long grain **white rice** (uncooked)
1/4 cups	**vegetable oil**
1/2	**onion**, chopped fine
1 teaspoon	granulated **garlic** (or 1 clove, minced)
3 cups	vegetable, chicken or beef **stock**
1 tablespoon	**tomato paste**
1 teaspoon	**salt**

Heat the oil in a heavy bottom frying pan. Lightly fry the onion and garlic in the pan until golden. Push to the side.

Add the rice and fry it until golden. Carefully and quickly add the stock, salt and tomato paste. (The hot pan will throw off steam, so have the lid ready to cover the pan.)

Cover and cook for 20 minutes over medium-low heat.

Makes 2 cups

RICE WITH CHILES

Arroz Con Rajas de Chile Poblano

Chef Pepe offers his favorite recipe for Mexican rice.
It tastes just the way his mom made it!

2 cups	long grain **rice**
⅓ cup	**olive oil**
2	ripe **tomatoes** cut in to chunks
¼ cup	white onion
2 teaspoons	chopped **garlic**
2 medium	**poblano chiles**, roasted, seeded, peeled
3 cups	warm **water**
1 teaspoon	**salt**

In a bowl, soak the rice in warm water to cover for 10 minutes. Drain well.

In a blender, blend tomatoes, garlic, onion and salt until it is a smooth paste.

Dice the chiles.

Heat oil in a heavy sauce pan. Sauté rice until golden brown (about 5 minutes).

Add the tomato mixture and the diced chiles. Add water and bring to a boil, stirring occasionally. Reduce heat to low. Stir once and cover. Simmer 10 minutes until rice is fluffy. Turn off the heat and let sit for 10 more minutes.

Makes 6 servings

BANANA RICE

Arroz Blanco con Platanos Fritos
(White Rice with Fried Plantains)

*Plantains look like bananas on steroids. This huge, solid fruit is a staple in
Latin America but can be hard to find elsewhere. If the exotic plantains are
not available, use large firm bananas. Chef Sergio remembers this
recipe from his home in Mexico.*

2 cups	long-grain **rice**
¹/₂ cup	**oil**
¹/₂	**onion**, cut in half
1 clove	**garlic**
5 cups	hot **water**
1 sprig	**parsley**
1 teaspoon	**salt**
1 whole	**serrano chile**
3	**plantains** or large firm bananas

Soak the rice for five minutes in warm water. Rinse well and drain.

Heat oil in a large skillet or casserole. (Adjust amount so it is about ¹/₂ inch deep.)
Carefully add the drained rice, onion and garlic. (There may be some serious spitting
when the wet rice hits the hot oil in the pan.)

Sauté until the rice is translucent and the grains separate. Pour off excess oil.

Add the hot water, parsley, salt and serrano chile. Bring to a boil and cover. Cook
over low heat for 25 minutes or until the rice is tender.

While the rice is cooking, peel the plantains and cut them lengthwise into strips ¹/₄
inch thick and 4 inches long. Heat oil in a skillet (again about ¹/₂ inch deep). Fry the
plantain strips on all sides until they are a dark golden color.

Serve the rice with strips of fried plantain on top.

Makes 4 servings

MAUI-MEX POTATOES

*Low-cal potatoes? Believe it! These boiled potatoes have no fat . . .
but add a filling "fried potato" taste to burritos.*

1 cup	russet **potatoes**,
	scrubbed and cut into ¼ inch cubes
1 teaspoon	**salt**
1 teaspoon	granulated **garlic**
1	**bay leaf**
1 tablespoon	fresh chopped **cilantro**
¼ cup	thin sliced white **onion**
	salt and **pepper** to taste

After scrubbing and dicing the potatoes, put the cubes in a bowl of ice water.
Bring the 2 cups of water, salt, garlic and bay leaf to a boil.
Drain off the ice water from the potatoes and carefully add them to the boiling water.
Cook potato cubes until just fork tender. Drain.
Place cooked potatoes in a bowl. While still warm, add fresh chopped cilantro and onion.
And salt and pepper to taste. Mix gently.

Fills 2 burritos

FRESH HOT
TORTILLA CHIPS

Totopos (crisply fried tortilla wedges)

*The Snack Food Association estimates that Americans ate
8.2 million pounds of tortilla chips . . . while watching the Super Bowl. Yikes!
Go for bagged chips if you are paying more attention to the tube than
to what you put in your mouth.*

*If you consider yourself a sophisticated snacker, please try this recipe
for Totopos. It's for folks who appreciate the finer things in life . . .
like fresh hot tortilla chips.*

8   day-old **corn tortillas**
    vegetable oil
    salt or **seasoned salt** to taste

Heat the oil to 350 degrees in a heavy skillet. The oil should be at least ½ inch deep.

Meanwhile, stack the tortillas and cut through the stack so the tortillas will be cut exactly in half. Continue cutting the stacks in half until they are cut into wedges the size you prefer. (The usual size is a wedge that is ⅛ of a tortilla.)

Gently slide some of the wedges into the hot oil. Cook only a few at a time to prevent crowding. Remove from the oil when they are lightly browned and crisp. Drain on paper towels and salt to taste. Serve with salsa and guacamole for a snack . . . or use them to scoop up rice and beans with a meal.

Serves 4

Dessert anyone?

Flour tortillas can also be cut and fried as described above. When done, lightly sprinkle them with cinnamon sugar and serve them for dessert alone or with a coffee flavored ice cream. (For best flavor, do not use the same oil used to fry the corn tortillas!)

MAUI TACOS MARINADE

(Use it on beef, chicken, pork, fish and vegetables)

*It's not just the grilling that makes the meat in our burritos
taste so amazing. Here is the real secret to the Maui Tacos grilled meats
and chicken . . . Maui Tacos Marinade! It can also be used for fish or vegetables.*

1 cup	**pineapple juice**
1 cup	fresh **lime juice**
1 tablespoon	**Hawaiian salt** (or Kosher salt)
1 tablespoon	dried **Mexican oregano**
6 cloves	**garlic**, chopped
1 teaspoon	fresh cracked **pepper**

Mix all the ingredients in a ceramic bowl or heavy gauge plastic bag.

Marinate meat or chicken in the mixture in the refrigerator for at least one hour (better yet . . . overnight.) Fish and vegetables only need to marinate about an hour.

Remove meat, chicken or veggies from marinade with a fork.

Grill over medium hot fire on the grill (charcoal should have a white ash coating.)

Meat can also be cooked in a grill pan, broiler or oven if grilling is not possible.

Do not save the marinade. It should be made fresh each time.

Makes 2 cups of marinade

GROUND BEEF TACO MEAT

*The secret Maui Tacos ground beef filling revealed! Did you guess
clove and pineapple juice as the secret ingredients?*

1 pound	lean **ground beef**
1 teaspoon	**salt**
½ teaspoon	ground **pepper**
1 teaspoon	granulated **garlic**
1 tablespoon	ground **cumin**
small pinch	ground **clove**
1 teaspoon	dried **oregano** (Mexican preferred)
3 ounces	**pineapple juice**
1 cup	**water**

Add all ingredients to heavy bottom pan. Bring to boil then simmer slowly for one
hour. Adjust for salt.

Enough filling for 4 large burritos

EASY SHREDDED COOKED CHICKEN MEAT

*When time is tight, you may be tempted to just go to Maui Tacos
for a burrito. That's cool. But these quick and easy options for shredded chicken
are almost as fast as a trip to the restaurant. The burrito fixings compliment
this shredded chicken perfectly, too.*

1 pound	**chicken** thighs or 2 chicken breasts
	salted water to cover
1	**onion**, roughly chopped
1 sprig	**cilantro** (optional)

Use a pot large enough to hold all the ingredients without crowding. Add enough water to cover the chicken; add the onion and cilantro. Bring the pot to a gentle boil. A lid is optional. Gently boil chicken thighs or breasts for 20 minutes. (Breasts may take an additional 15 minutes). Leave meat to cool in the broth. (Reserve the broth for other recipes requiring broth or water . . . especially Mexican rice.)

Remove any skin or bones and shred the chicken meat.

Makes enough for 2 large burritos

Really in a hurry?

Use shredded meat from a fully cooked chicken from the deli, Costco or convenience section of the supermarket.

SHREDDED CHICKEN, BEEF OR PORK

Chef Pepe uses this traditional "Tinga-Puebla" recipe to put extra flavor into his shredded meat dishes. The cooked meat is finished in a chipotle-tomato mixture. Try this recipe with a whole chicken . . . or a small beef or pork roast. The meat can be used in burritos, tacos, salads or even sandwiches . . . and it goes quickly.

1 pound	**chicken, beef** or **pork**
2	**bay leaves**
3 ounces	**olive oil**
4 cloves	**garlic**, chopped
1	**onion**, sliced
1 teaspoon	**cumin**
1 teaspoon	**black pepper**
1 teaspoon	**salt**
2	**tomatoes**, chopped
3 tablespoons	**tomato paste**
3	**chiles chipotle** in adobo

Cover the meat with water in a pot. Add the bay leaves. Bring to a boil over high heat, then reduce heat to medium.

Gently simmer as follows: Chicken (thighs or breast) for ½ hour, Beef or Pork for 1 hour. Check at this point for tenderness with a fork. Continue simmering if necessary.

After the meat is tender, remove it from the broth and let cool. Save the broth. Shred the meat with your fingers or two forks. Discard any bone, skin or excess fat.

In a different pot heated over high heat, add olive oil and garlic. Sauté for a minute reducing heat if it starts to smoke. Add onion and sauté it until caramelized.

Stir in the cumin, black pepper and salt. Add tomatoes, tomato paste and 2 cups of reserved broth (or chicken broth). Put the chipotles in a blender or food processor with a bit of stock and process until it is a chunky paste consistency. Add it to the pot and stir to mix ingredients.

Add the shredded meat. Let it simmer for 10 minutes.

Use this shredded meat hot from the pot in recipes calling for shredded meat. Refrigerate any leftovers promptly.

Enough filling for 4 burritos

CHILE VERDE

Try this in your next burrito or taco. This delicious pork is tender and juicy.
Brown the meat well for good color and a "roasted" flavor.

3 pounds	fat trimmed **pork butt**
¼ cup	**vegetable oil**
1	**bay leaf**
2 cups	**water**
	Chile Verde Sauce (recipe follows)

Cut pork into one inch cubes. Sauté pork in sauté pan with vegetable oil.
Brown meat well on all sides. Add bay leaf and water to the pan. Simmer for 15 minutes.
Drain any excess water from the pan. Cover meat with Chile Verde Sauce. Simmer for 15 minutes or until fork tender. Adjust for salt.

Chile Verde Sauce:

In a blender, pulse to process:

3	fresh **jalapeños** stemmed and seeded
½ cup	**white onion**, chopped
⅛ cup	fresh chopped **cilantro**
2 cloves	fresh **garlic**
1 teaspoon	**salt**
2 cups	fresh or canned diced **tomatillos**
½ teaspoon	ground **pepper**
½ cup	**water**

Blend the sauce until smooth.

Enough filling for 6 burritos

ENCHILADA SAUCE

This good-looking sauce gets its deep red color from the chilies, not tomatoes.
It's equally tasty in a baking dish full of cheese enchiladas or drenched over a naked
burrito. (Hence the term "Wet Burrito" we use around the restaurant.)
Enhance the flavor even more by dry roasting the ancho chilies
in a cast iron skillet until they are dark and fragrant.

Sauce:

2	whole dried **ancho chilies,** stem and seeds removed
1 quart	**water** or vegetable stock
2	**bay leaves**
1 tablespoon	granulated **garlic**
1 tablespoon	ground **pepper**
1 tablespoon	ground **cumin**
1 teaspoon	**salt**
¼ cup	ground New Mexico **chile powder**
2 tablespoons	**tomato paste**
1 clove	fresh **garlic**
¼ cup	**white onion**, coarsely diced

Roux:

1 cup	unbleached **flour**
½ cup	**vegetable oil**

Dry roast the ancho chiles in a frying pan (no oil) over medium high heat until they get a dark color. Remove from heat.

Blend all of the sauce ingredients (not the roux ingredients) together until smooth in a blender. Place the blended ingredients into a pot.

Bring sauce to a simmer over medium heat.

Meanwhile make a roux by blending the flour and vegetable oil with a wire whisk in a small pot. Add more flour or oil as necessary. Roux should be smooth and fairly thick.

Heat the roux over medium heat until it turns a very light golden brown.

Add ½ the roux mixture to the red sauce. Continue cooking the sauce for 20 minutes, sauce should be getting thicker the longer it cooks. Add more roux if it is not thick enough. Sauce should coat the back of a spoon.

Cook for 20 more minutes, adding more water or stock if it gets too thick.

Serving Suggestion: Top a single burrito . . . or a pan of burritos with some of this sauce and lots of cheese. Run it under a broiler or put the pan in a 350 degree oven until the cheese melts.

Makes 4 cups of sauce

THE MAUI-MEX SALSA BAR

Psssst . . . No lie, brah. Here are the secret recipes for
Maui Tacos salsas. Like your salsa fruity and mild? Got it.
Prefer it scorching HOT and robust with bits of roasted peppers?
It's here, too. All the recipes are adapted for the home kitchen.
Each salsa is based on the best-loved favorites at the
Maui Tacos salsa bar in the restaurant.

SALSAS AND SAUCES

⚡ = *mild*   ⚡⚡ = *medium hot*   ⚡⚡⚡ = *go in at your own risk*

FRESH PINEAPPLE GINGER   28   ◢
SALSA (fruity, with a hint of mint)

AVOCADO SALSA (this is NOT guacamole)   29   ◢

MAUI-MEX GREEN TOMATILLO   31   ◢ ◢
SALSA (use fresh or canned tomatillos)

PEPE'S ROASTED ARBOL   32   ◢
AND TOMATILLO SALSA

PEPE'S SALSA FOR CARNITAS   33   ◢ ◢

GUACAMOLE

FRONT STREET MANGO GUACAMOLE   34

GUACAMOLE DE LA MISTECA   36

When you can't make it to a Maui Tacos restaurant, you can create a home version of our salsa bar for any meal that includes a burrito or taco. Try a couple of different salsas for a simple dinner at home. For a party, however, go with at least four varieties.

Homemade salsas will keep in the refrigerator for up to a week. The guacamole is best if it's made just before it is served. Even if your salsa bar is in Minnesota in winter, it's a good idea to keep the perishable stuff cold . . . sour cream, chopped raw ingredients like onions and cilantro, and cheeses. Prepare them in separate decorative bowls—cover with plastic wrap and hold them in the fridge. Bring them out just before serving time.

HOME-VERSION SALSA BAR GOODIES

- a variety of salsas— red, green, hot, mild
- guacamole
- warm corn chips
- fresh chopped cilantro
- sour cream

- diced Maui onion
- diced mango
- black olives
- fire roasted corn kernels
- diced red bell pepper
- shredded Cheddar, Mexican and/or Jack cheese

- sliced jalapeños
- diced avocado
- chopped tomatoes
- shredded lettuce
- lemon or lime wedges
- whatever!

HOLA ALOHA SALSA®

Hola Aloha (hello, hello?) is a basic medium-hot cooked salsa.
Here at Maui Tacos it is the #1 choice at the salsa bar. We base this
statistic strictly on how often we refill its bowl.
This stuff is so popular, some people were filling up dozens of those tiny
plastic cups we have out at the salsa bar and making a mess.
So, we now offer Hola Aloha in a bottle to go.
Go figure . . . It's one of the easiest salsas to make!
Here is the recipe so make a batch at home.

2 cups	**tomatoes**, quartered
2	**jalapeño peppers**, stemmed and seeded
1 cup	**onion**, diced
3	**garlic cloves**
1 cup	**water**
¹⁄₂ cup	**cilantro** leaves

Put all the ingredients (except cilantro) in a heavy saucepan. Boil gently for two minutes. Remove pan from heat and let the mixture cool.

Pour the mixture into a blender and add the cilantro. Blend the salsa by pulsing repeatedly . . . but don't overblend. It tastes best with a bit of texture.

Chill for 1 hour before serving.

Makes about 3 cups

HULA HEAT!®

A Chile Arbol Salsa

"Forget the hula, that's a fire dance going on in my mouth,"
said one of our satisfied customers. Yes, it's hot, but you can't stay
away from this fire. The secret? Dried Hawaiian Chile peppers or Chile Arbol—
small hot peppers—are roasted to release a rich dark essence.
We don't remove the seeds of the chile when we want an even hotter salsa.
Use ripe tomatoes and fresh tomatillos if possible, but canned can be substituted.

12	dried **Hawaiian chile peppers** or **chile arbol,** stemmed and seeded
1 teaspoon	**vegetable oil**
1 cup	fresh **tomatoes,** quartered
1/2 cup	fresh **tomatillos,** quartered
1/4 cup	**onion,** diced
2	**garlic cloves**
1/2 cup	**water**
	salt and pepper to taste

Heat oil in a pan over medium heat. Toast the prepared chiles and garlic in the oil until they turn a dark "chocolate" color. Let the mixture cool.

In a separate pot, cook tomatillos, tomatoes and onion in the water for 5 minutes. Remove pot from heat and let this mixture cool.

Add all ingredients to blender. Blend for 5 seconds. (There will be tiny specs of the toasted chile dotting the sauce.) Chill before serving.

Makes about 2 cups.

MAUI-MEX PICO DE GALLO

Here is our motto: Fresh, uncooked salsa demands the freshest ingredients.
Use the best red ripe tomatoes in the market . . . and sweet Maui onion
if it is available. Although this recipe can be made with canned tomatoes
in a pinch, it will be a completely different salsa.

2 cups	fresh diced **tomato**
¼ cup	fresh chopped **cilantro leaves**
½ cup	freshly diced Maui **onion**
¼ cup	fresh squeezed **lime juice**
¼ cup	fresh **orange juice**
	salt and **pepper** to taste
2	**jalapeño peppers,** chopped (seeds and all)

Mix all ingredients except the salt, pepper and jalapeño together in a bowl.
Add the salt, pepper and jalapeño to taste.
Let salsa sit for at least 15 minutes before using.
Use fresh . . . or make it ahead and refrigerate.

Makes about 3 cups

MAUI PINEAPPLE PASSION SALSA®

We had a lot of pineapple to work with on Maui, so we threw some in the salsa.
It turned out to be a stroke of culinary genius. Fresh pineapple gives this
salsa a zippy fruit flavor that's delightful. Canned pineapple will work, too.
Look for the 100% Maui Grown label and help our local economy.
Regulate the heat of this salsa by adjusting the amount of jalapeño pepper you use.
Served it chilled, but—with two jalapeño peppers—it's still going to be HOT!

½ cup	fresh **pineapple,** small bite-sized pieces
½ cup	**tomatillo,** fresh or drained whole canned
½ cup	**pineapple juice**
2	**jalapeño** peppers, stemmed and seeded
¼ cup	fresh **cilantro leaves**
1 clove	**garlic,** whole, peeled
1 teaspoon	Mexican **oregano,** dried
	salt and **pepper** to taste

Place ½ of the pineapple in a pot. Be sure to remove all papery outer peel from the tomatillos and chop roughly. Add all of the tomatillo and pineapple juice.

Cook for 5 minutes over medium heat. Cool. Set aside in a glass or ceramic bowl.

Place remaining ingredients into blender and puree for 5 seconds. Combine with cooled mixture in the bowl. Chill thoroughly before serving.

Makes about 2 cups

MAUI FIRE DANCER® SMOKEY CHIPOTLE PINEAPPLE SALSA

Sweet and smokey . . . we think it's a perfect blend of flavors.
Pineapple gives this salsa its understated sweetness, while the chipotle,
a dried smoked jalapeño from the Yucatan area of Mexico,
gives it a satisfying musky flavor. "Chipotle en Adobo" means the
chile is cooked with a tomato sauce. Canned Chipotle en Adobo
can be found in the Mexican section of your market.

1 can	**chipotle en adobo** (7 ¾ ounces)
1 cup	fresh **tomatoes,** quartered
2	**garlic cloves**
¹/₂ cup	**onion,** diced
¹/₂ cup	**pineapple juice**
	salt and **pepper** to taste

Mix ingredients (except salt and pepper) in a heavy pan and cook for 5 minutes.
Remove tomato skins from the mixture at this point if desired. Cool mixture.
Pour mixture into a blender. Blend for 5 seconds. Add salt and pepper to taste.
Chill before serving.

Makes about 2 cups

MANGO PINEAPPLE SALSA

We suggest you take a tub of this to the beach . . .
or scoop it up with tortilla chips on the lanai with a cold drink.
Try this sweet salsa with chicken and fish, too.

½ cup	fresh **mango,** diced
½ cup	fresh **pineapple,** diced
½ cup	fresh **tomato,** diced
½ cup	sweet **onion,** diced
¼ cup	fresh **jicama,** diced
⅛ cup	fresh **cilantro leaves,** minced
1 teaspoon	fresh grated **ginger**
1 tablespoon	fresh **mint,** minced
1	**lime,** juice only
	fresh **chile pepper, salt** and **pepper** to taste

Mix all ingredients together in a bowl.
Can be served chilled or at room temperature.
Refrigerate any leftover salsa.

Makes about 2 cups

FRESH PINEAPPLE GINGER SALSA

Ooooh, so many flavors dancing in your mouth.
This is not a typical salsa (no tomatoes and it's very smooth),
but this green sauce adds a punch of flavor and color
when served over grilled chicken or fish.

1 cup	fresh **pineapple**, diced (¼″ × ¼″)
1 cup	fresh **tomato,** diced (¼″ × ¼″)
2	**limes,** juice only
1	**garlic clove,** chopped
¼ cup	**cilantro leaves**, shredded
1 tablespoon	fresh chopped **mint**
1 tablespoon	fresh chopped **ginger**
1	fresh **Hawaiian chile pepper**, diced
1 teaspoon	**Hawaiian salt** (or Kosher)
½ teaspoon	fresh cracked **pepper**

Put first four ingredients in a bowl and mix. Stir in the rest of the ingredients to taste.

Makes about 2 cups of sauce

ELEGANT AVOCADO SALSA

Turn a naked burrito into a something spectacular!
Not at all like guacamole, this green sauce is gorgeous when drizzled
over a burrito resting on a chilled plate pooled with a red salsa like
Tomato Cilantro Salsa. Garnish with fresh cilantro leaves . . .

½ cup	ripe **avocado,** skin and seed removed
½ cup	**tomatillo** (fresh or canned)
2	**jalapeño peppers,** stemmed and seeded
2	**garlic cloves** (peeled)
1 cup	fresh **cilantro leaves**
½ cup	**water**
2 tablespoons	pickled **jalapeño juice**
¼ cup	fresh squeezed **lime juice**
	salt and **pepper** to taste

Fresh tomatillos need to have their papery outer shell removed. If using canned tomatillos, just drain them. Chop the tomatillos roughly.

Put all ingredients into blender and puree until very smooth. Add additional water if needed. (Salsa should coat a back of a spoon.)

Remove salsa to a glass or ceramic bowl. Chill thoroughly.

Makes about 2 cups

The first Maui Tacos opened in Napili in 1993 . . .
and brought Maui-Mex to the world!

MAUI-MEX GREEN TOMATILLO SALSA

No, they aren't tiny green tomatoes. Tomatillos are the main ingredient in lots of salsas, though. Fresh or canned, they give this salsa its distinctive flavor and green color. This salsa is especially good with egg, potato or pork based recipes.

1 cup	**tomatillos**
2	**garlic cloves**
1/2 cup	**onion**
2	**jalapeño peppers,** stemmed and seeded
1/2 cup	**water**
2 tablespoons	fresh squeezed **lime juice**
1/2 cup	fresh **cilantro leaves**
	salt and **pepper** to taste

If using *fresh* tomatillos, remove the papery husks and chop them. Roughly chop the garlic, onion and jalapeño. Bring garlic, onion, jalapeño, fresh tomatillos* and water to a boil in a pot. Simmer for 5 minutes. Allow the mixture to cool.

*Do not cook canned tomatillos. Drain and add them to the mixture in the blender now.

Place the cooled mixture in a blender. Add the lime juice and cilantro leaves.
Puree for 5 seconds. Add salt and pepper to taste
Serve chilled. Store in the refrigerator.

Makes about 2 cups

PEPE'S ROASTED ARBOL AND TOMATILLO SALSA

Chile Arbol are those orange-red, skinny and very hot chile peppers.
In Hawaii, similar chiles grow wild along the road
and in backyard gardens. Roasting the chile intensifies the flavor.
Being so small, peeling the skins off would be time consuming.
No worries . . . bits of the roasted vegetable skins can
add texture and flavor to this salsa.

20	whole **tomatillos**
1	**tomato**
1	**garlic clove**
15	**Hawaiian chiles** or **chile arbol**
¼ cup	**water**
	salt to **taste**

Roast husked tomatillos, tomato and chiles on a flat pan about 6 inches under the broiler element or gas oven flame. When the skins start to turn a blackish color and "lift" away from the flesh of the vegetables, be ready to pull them out of the oven. Remove as much of the blackened skins as desired. The blackened skin adds color, flavor and texture.

In a blender, add the water and garlic. Pulse the garlic a few times, then add the roasted vegetables. Blend to a chunky consistency. Add salt to taste.

Makes about 3 cups

PEPE'S SALSA FOR CARNITAS

This is Chef Pepe's favorite salsa to serve with carnitas . . .
but don't restrict this salsa to ONLY carnitas.
It is delightful served with lots of other Maui-Mex dishes.

2	**garlic cloves**
1/4 cup	**water**
1/4 cup	**white vinegar**
1/8 cup	**jalapeño juice**
	(reserved from canned chiles below)
3	whole **tomatoes**
10	whole **tomatillos**
4 ounces	**jalapeño,** canned "en escabeche" style
	(pickled with vegetables)
1/4 teaspoon	**oregano**
1	**onion,** diced
	salt to taste

In a blender, combine garlic with water, vinegar and jalapeño juice. Blend to a very smooth liquid.

Cut tomatoes and tomatillos into small chunks and add them to the blender. Add the jalapeño en escabeche. Pulse ingredients in blender to a chunky consistency.

Add diced onion and oregano. Salt to taste.

Makes 3 cups

FRONT STREET MANGO GUACAMOLE

Think it's impossible to improve upon traditional guacamole?
Wait until you try this version. Mark uses Hayden mangos from his backyard
in Lahaina. You can use any variety available to you . . .

2 cups	ripe **avocado** (use 3–4 large Haas or Sharwill)
1 cup	**Maui onion** or any sweet onion (diced ¼ inch square)
1 cup	**tomato** (fresh, ripe and diced ¼ inch square)
1	**mango** (fresh, ripe and diced ¼ inch square)
½ cup	**lemon juice,** fresh squeezed
4 tablespoons	**cilantro,** minced
¼ teaspoon	**nutmeg,** grated
1 tablespoon	**jalapeño** or **serrano pepper,** minced
	vegetable oil
	optional: salt and **pepper** to taste

Gather and prepare all ingredients . . . this assembles FAST. Dice the Maui onion, tomato and mango. Set aside. Cut the avocados in half and remove the pits. Use a large spoon to scoop out the avocado meat into a heavy bowl. Sprinkle lemon juice over the avocado meat to keep it from turning brown. Have cilantro and nutmeg ready.

Sear the jalapeño or serrano pepper in a small amount of salted vegetable oil in a frying pan until the skin blisters. Chop coarsely. (You may use more or less than a tablespoon depending on your heat tolerance level! The charred pepper skin can be included in the guacamole for flavor and texture . . . or it can be removed before chopping.)

Mash the avocado meat and mix all ingredients together in a ceramic bowl. Season to taste with salt and pepper if desired. Chill for two hours.

Serve with chips . . . or as a topping for salads, sandwiches or tacos.

Makes approximately 3 cups

Chef's Tip: Mango Made Easy

It's really easy to cut the mango into the cubes. Honest! Use a very sharp knife. Slice the fresh unpeeled mango in half (from top to bottom) all the way around. Pull each half free of the large seed . . . using the knife if needed to help free the flesh.

Score the inside of the mango halves with the knife making ¼ inch squares. Turn each mango half inside out . . . and cut the cubes free.

Frozen mango chunks work in this recipe, too. Thaw and dice the fruit into ¼ inch squares.

Lahaina Maui Tacos

GUACAMOLE DE LA MISTECA

Chef Sergio offers up a traditional guacamole recipe . . . pure and simple. Rather than mixing in tomatoes, he serves them on the side for a colorful presentation.

Try making guacamole with an authentic stone mortar . . . or molcajete . . . and serve it immediately right from the stone bowl. If you are making it ahead, a few drops of lime juice will keep the guacamole from turning dark.

Guacamole:	4	large, ripe **avocados**
	1 cup	minced **onion**
	4	**serrano** or **chiles arbol,** minced
	¹/₂ cup	**cilantro leaves,** finely chopped
		salt to taste
Garnish:	¹/₂	ripe **tomato,** diced
	¹/₄ cup	minced **onion**
	4–6 sprigs	**cilantro** with stems

To make the guacamole: Peel and pit the avocados. Scoop out the meat with a spoon and begin to mash the pulp in a bowl. Add salt to taste. Add minced onion, chiles and cilantro leaves. Continue mashing until the guacamole is thick and still a bit lumpy.

Presentation: Place the guacamole in a serving bowl and garnish with the diced tomato, onion and cilantro sprigs. Serve immediately with plenty of corn tortilla chips or totopos (crisply fried tortilla wedges) and a selection of salsas.

Makes about 3 cups

MAUI-MEX BURRITOS

Burritos are what made Maui Tacos famous.
Our customers say burritos are the perfect meal to
take to the beach and most Maui Tacos are so close to
the ocean they are located in a tsunami zone!

Just wrap up all the fresh fillings in the tortilla and
wrap it all again in foil. Neat, nourishing . . .
and no sand getting in there, eh?

When dinning at home, try a "wet" burrito—
essentially a "naked" burrito covered with
warm mellow enchilada sauce. These make a substantial
knife-and-fork kind of meal. If you really want to
impress guests, go for the gourmet burritos.

BASIC SURF BURRITOS

THE LAHAINA BURRITO (Chicken or Steak)   40

THE NAPILI BURRITO (Chicken or Steak)   41

THE HONOLII BURRITO (Ground Beef)   42

THE SHACKS (Chicken or Steak)   43

THE LA PEROUSE BURRITO (Chicken or Steak)   44

THE DUMPS BURRITO (Chicken or Steak)   45

THE HOOKIPA BURRITO (Fresh Fish)   46

THE HAIKU BURRITO (Vegetarian with Potatoes)   47

THE PAIA BURRITO (Salad Burrito)   48

GOURMET BURRITOS

INTERNATIONAL BURRITOS

These burritos are dedicated to the surfers from around the world
who gather in Hawaii to surf the legendary waves.
Talk about multi-cultural eating. Sushi in a tortilla? Why not!

BREAKFAST BURRITOS

These burritos are just as delicious and easy to eat
in your car on the way to work . . . as they are on the
beach at sunrise waiting for the perfect wave.

For a burrito that tastes like it's just been rolled in a Maui Tacos kitchen . . . use the recipes in the Basics Chapter for beans and rice. Chef Mark, Chef Pepe and Chef Sergio have included their favorite recipes for these Mexican mainstays. Canned beans and even prepared salsas will work in a real pinch. As long as you didn't burn the beans . . . the warm tortilla makes everything taste great.

Go shopping for fresh and authentic ingredients. Farmer's markets often have hard-to-find Mexican style cheeses, homemade tortillas and the freshest tomatoes and cilantro. It's a culinary treasure hunt when we go to see what is new in the Mexican food section or specialty markets.

Experiment with ingredients. If you like the taste of it, go for it. Don't be afraid to add some unusual ingredients—from plain yogurt to a bit of fresh corn—in a burrito. You can name the burrito YOU create after your favorite surf spot.

Save yourself some prep time in the kitchen and serve any these burritos family style. Have a stack of warm tortillas in the center of the table. Put the fillings in decorative bowls with serving spoons. Each person can customize their burrito. Suddenly it's no problem if someone wants mild Oxaca cheese, while someone else wants shredded jalapeño jack cheese!

THE LAHAINA BURRITO

(Meat, Rice, Cheese and Guacamole)

This burrito proves the KISS adage. (Keep It Simple, Señor.)
It is the most popular burrito at Maui Tacos.
When grilling the meat, it's easy to double the amount
suggested in the recipe and refrigerate leftovers for
quick burritos later in the week.

2	flour **tortillas,** 12-inch (any flavor)
1 pound	**chicken breast** or **steak** (fillet, top round, etc.) seasoned with Hawaiian or kosher salt and cracked pepper
1 cup	Maui Tacos **rice** (page 8)
¹/₂ cup	**guacamole** (page 36)
¹/₂ cup	shredded **jack** and **cheddar cheese** Hola Aloha Sauce, to taste (page 22)

To grill the meat: Use a grill pan under a broiler . . . or grill outdoors using kiawe wood or charcoal briquettes. Season the chicken breast or steak with Hawaiian salt and cracked pepper. Cook to the degree of doneness preferred. Remove to a platter. Slice the steak thinly or slice/pull the chicken from the bone. Set the meat aside and keep warm.

To assemble: Warm the tortillas. Cover with foil (to keep them warm and pliable) and work with them one at a time. Review the Tortilla Warming and Burrito Assembly Instructions in the "How to Maui-Mex" chapter if necessary.

Layer the rice down the center of each tortilla and top with meat. Top the meat with guacamole, cheese and salsa to taste.

Roll the tortillas tightly around the fillings. Wrap each burrito in pre-cut foil sheets if desired.

Makes 2 burritos

THE NAPILI BURRITO
(Meat, Rice, Black Beans and Cheese)

Nothing beats chicken or steak fresh from the grill on this burrito.
This is a hearty and satisfying burrito.

2	flour **tortillas,** 12-inch (any flavor)
1 cup	grilled **chicken** or **steak**
1 cup	Maui Tacos **rice**
1 cup	**black beans**
¹/₂ cup	shredded **cheddar cheese**
	salsa, to taste

To grill the meat: Cook on a grill pan, under a broiler . . . or outdoors on a grill using kiawe wood or charcoal. Season the chicken breast or steak with Hawaiian salt and cracked pepper. Cook to the degree of doneness preferred. Remove to a platter. Slice the meat thinly or pull the chicken from the bone. Set the meat aside and keep warm.

Warm the tortillas. Cover with foil (to keep them warm) and work with them one at a time.

Layer the rice and beans in the center of each tortilla and top with meat.

Top with cheese and salsa to taste.

Roll the tortillas as shown on page 111. Wrap each burrito tightly in foil if desired.

Makes 2 burritos

Chef's Tip: We don't want to dictate your salsa! At the restaurant, customers can select their favorite salsa from the Maui Tacos Salsa Bar. So, we have included the recipes of our salsa favorites in the Salsa chapter of this book. The recipes are quick to prepare, taste fresh and keep in the refrigerator for days.

HONOLII BURRITO

(The Ground Beef Burrito)

When grilling the meat for your burrito is not an option,
this ground beef burrito is an excellent choice.

2	flour **tortillas,** 12-inch (any flavor)
1 cup	**ground beef**
1 cup	Maui Tacos **rice** (page 8)
1 cup	**black beans** (page 5 or canned)
1/2 cup	shredded **cheddar cheese**
1/3 cup	**sour cream**
1 cup	shredded **lettuce**
	salsa, to taste

Warm the tortillas. Cover with foil (to keep them warm) and work with them one at a time.

Cook the ground beef in a frying pan. Drain off excess fat (or use recipe on page 16).

Layer rice, beans and cooked beef in the center of each tortilla.

Top with cheese, sour cream, salsa and lettuce.

Roll the tortillas as shown on page 111. Wrap each burrito tightly in foil if desired.

Makes 2 burritos

SHACKS BURRITO
(Meat, pinto beans and cheese)

This is the basic burrito. NOT EVEN RICE!
Because sometimes a simple burrito is best . . .

2	flour **tortillas,** 12-inch (any flavor)
1 cup	whole cooked **pinto beans**
1 cup	cooked **chicken** or **steak**
$^1/_2$ cup	shredded **cheddar cheese**

Meat: Follow one of the meat filling recipes in the "Maui-Mex Basics" chapter.

Warm the tortillas. Cover with foil (to keep them warm.) Work with them one at a time.

Layer the beans, meat and cheese in the center of each tortilla.

Roll as shown on page 111. Wrap tightly in foil if desired.

Makes 2 burritos

LA PEROUSE

(The Works!)

An awesome "South Swell" of a burrito. Better be hungry for this one.

2	flour **tortillas,** 12-inch (any flavor)
1 cup	grilled **chicken breast meat**
1 cup	sliced grilled **steak**
1 cup	whole cooked **pinto** or **black beans**
1 cup	**rice,** cooked any style
1 cup	shredded **lettuce**
1/3 cup	**sour cream**
1/3 cup	**guacamole**
	salsa, to taste

To grill the meat: Cook on a grill pan, under a broiler . . . or outdoors on a grill using kiawe wood or charcoal. Season the chicken breast or steak with Hawaiian salt and cracked pepper. Cook to the degree of doneness preferred. Remove to a platter. Slice the steak thinly or pull the chicken from the bone. Set the meat aside and keep warm.

Warm the tortillas. Cover with foil (to keep them warm) and work with them one at a time.

Layer chicken, steak, beans and rice in the center of each tortilla. Top with lettuce, sour cream, guacamole and salsa. Roll and wrap tightly in foil if desired.

Makes 2 burritos

THE DUMPS BURRITO

(Meat, Rice and Beans Burrito)

Try the Maui Tacos Rice and Black Beans recipes for this burrito.

2	flour **tortillas,** 12-inch (any flavor)
1 cup	**chicken** or **steak**
1 cup	**rice** (cooked any style)
3/4 cup	pinto or **black beans**

Use one of the recipes in the Maui-Mex Basics chapter for the meat.

Warm the tortillas. Cover with foil (to keep them warm) and work with them one at a time.

Layer the chicken or steak, beans and rice in the center of each tortilla. Top with lettuce, sour cream, guacamole and salsa. Roll and wrap tightly in foil if desired.

Makes 2 burritos

THE HOOKIPA

(The Fresh Island Fish Burrito)

Gone fishing lately?
This simple burrito needs the freshest fish for the best flavor.

2	flour **tortillas,** 12-inch (any flavor)
½ pound	**ahi** or other fresh fish
1 cup	Maui Tacos **rice**
1 cup	**black beans**
⅓ cup	**sour cream**
	salsa, to taste

Grill the fish or sauté it quickly in a non-stick pan over medium high heat. Break the cooked fish into bite size chunks making sure to remove any bones or skin.

Warm the tortillas. Cover with foil (to keep them warm) and work with them one at a time.

Layer ½ of the rice and beans in the center area of each tortilla. Distribute the fish over the beans and rice. Top the fillings with sour cream and salsa to taste.

Roll the tortilla around the fillings. Wrap in foil or serve on a plate with a "fresh greens" salad.

Makes 2 burritos

THE HAIKU BURRITO

(A Very Satisfying Vegetarian Burrito)

This one is especially good with additional cheese melted over the top of the finished burrito. Place the folded burrito on a heatproof plate, sprinkle shredded cheese over the top and put in the oven or toaster oven just until the cheese melts.

2	flour **tortillas,** 12-inch (any flavor)
1 cup	cooked **potato** chunks
	(see Maui Tacos Potatoes on page 12)
1 cup	**black beans**
1/2 cup	shredded **jack** or **cheddar cheese**
1 cup	shredded **lettuce**
1/3 cup	**sour cream**
	salsa, to taste

Warm the tortillas. Cover with foil (to keep them warm) and work with them one at a time.

Layer 1/2 of the potatoes, beans, cheese, lettuce in the center of each tortilla.

Top with sour cream and salsa to taste. Roll the tortillas. Wrap each in a sheet of foil if desired.

Makes 2 burritos

THE PAIA BURRITO

(The Salad Burrito)

We serve up a lot of these at Maui Tacos.
A extra special touch is to mix a sprinkling of
fresh cilantro leaves or sunflower sprouts in with the lettuce.

2	flour **tortillas,** 12-inch (any flavor)
2 cups	shredded **lettuce** (any kind)
1 cup	**rice**
1 cup	cooked **black beans**
$^1/_2$ cup	fresh diced **tomatoes**
$^1/_2$ cup	**guacamole**
	salsa to taste

Warm the tortillas. Cover with foil (to keep them warm) and work with them one at a time.

Layer $^1/_2$ of the lettuce, rice, beans and tomatoes in the center of each tortilla. Top with guacamole and salsa to taste. Roll the tortillas as shown on page 111. Wrap in foil if desired.

Makes 2 burritos

THE FRIED BURRITO
(Bean and Meat)

This crispy burrito is rolled tight—so the tortilla can hold in the filling while it fries. Garnish with guacamole, sour cream and salsa . . . and your patriotic burrito will be draped in the colors of the Mexican flag!

4	flour **tortillas** (10–12 inch size)
1 cup	**refried beans** (see page 4)
1 cup	cooked **rice**
2 cups	cooked **chicken** or **beef,** shredded
	vegetable oil for frying
	salsa, guacamole and **sour cream** for garnish

Use ¼ of the beans, rice and meat in each tortilla. Put them in the center of a warm tortilla as shown on page 111. Roll as tightly as possible without splitting or tearing the tortilla.

Select a high-sided frying pan and pour in two inches of vegetable oil. Heat the oil to 350 degrees. Use tongs to carefully place the burrito(s) in the hot oil with the flaps down.

Fry the burritos gently, turning them over once so that all sides are golden brown. Remove from hot oil and place on dry paper towel to drain.

Put burritos on serving plate. Top each with your favorite salsa, a dollop of sour cream and some guacamole.

Makes 4 burritos

Chef's Tip: Do not crowd burritos in the pan. Fry one or two at a time, if necessary, for even browning.

DIG-ME BURRITO

(Potato, Rice and Beans Burrito)

*This burrito can go from "mild mannered" to
"wildly spicy" depending on the salsa you select.
Make everyone happy by offering a selection of salsas and let
them "roll their own" burritos.*

2	flour **tortillas,** 12-inch (any flavor)
1 cup	cooked **potato** chunks (see Maui Tacos Potatoes page 12)
³/₄ cup	**rice**
³/₄ cup	**black beans**
	salsa, to taste

Warm the tortillas. Cover with foil (to keep them warm) and work with them one at a time.

Layer ¹/₂ of the potato chunks, rice and beans in the center of each tortilla.

Top these filling ingredients with salsa to taste. Roll the tortilla. Wrap each in a sheet of foil if desired.

Makes 2 burritos

KIAWE GRILLED STEAK BURRITO

Man, this is good eating! If you can't get kiawe wood, no worries.
Mesquite charcoal will give a similar smoky flavor to the meat.

1 pound	**steak** (fillet, flank, top round, etc.)
	Hawaiian salt (or kosher salt)
	and **cracked pepper**
1	**onion,** cut into thick slices
1	**potato,** cut into chunks
1 cup	sliced **mushrooms**
2	flour **tortillas,** 12-inch (any flavor)
1/2 cup	shredded **cheese**
2 ounces	**chipotle sauce,** or to taste
2 teaspoons	fresh **cilantro** leaves, chopped

Season the steak with Hawaiian salt and cracked pepper. Prepare the grill! When the kiawe wood or charcoal is covered with white ash, sear the steak on both sides and continue to cook until medium rare. Grill the onion slices for a minute on each side. Remove the meat and onion slices to a platter. Slice the meat thinly, set aside and keep warm.

Cook the potatoes according to the Maui Tacos Potato recipe on page 12. Push aside and sauté the mushrooms in the same pan.

Warm the tortillas. Cover with foil (to keep them warm) and work with them one at a time.

Layer the potatoes and mushrooms in the center of each tortilla. Distribute the sliced steak and onion evenly over it. Top with cheese, chipolte sauce and cilantro.

Roll the tortillas as shown on page 111. Wrap in foil if desired . . . or serve on a plate as an entrée with a salad. This burrito can be eaten with a knife and fork!

Makes 2 burritos

Chef's Tip: Toss a second steak on the grill and refrigerate the extra meat for burritos another day. Use the meat cold . . . or reheat it just before using in the burrito. The flavor is still unbeatable and steaks are often priced lower when purchased in bulk.

LAHAINA SUNSET BURRITO

(Grilled Chicken Breast with Mango Pesto Sauce)

This burrito, bursting with marinated grilled chicken breast,
is a favorite at Maui Tacos restaurants . . . and at Mark's
"private party" catering jobs in the islands.

Marinade:	1 cup	**pineapple juice**
	1 cup	**lime juice**
	2 tablespoons	dried **oregano,** Mexican preferred
	2 tablespoons	**garlic,** fresh minced or granulated
	1 tablespoon	each **salt** and **pepper,** fresh ground

Also needed for the burritos:	1 pound	**chicken breast,** boned and skinned
	4	flour **tortillas,** 12-inch (any style or flavor)
	1 cup	**Maui Tacos rice** (See recipe on page 8)
		Mango Pesto Salsa or other salsa
	1 pound	fresh **spinach leaves,** washed, dried and julienne sliced

Mix marinade ingredients in a glass or ceramic bowl large enough to hold the chicken breast(s). Marinate the chicken in the marinade for 24 hours in the refrigerator. It's best to grill the chicken over kiawe or mesquite on an outdoor grill, but the broiler or an indoor grill will work. Grill chicken until juices run clear. Dice the chicken into 1 inch by ¼ inch pieces. Set aside and keep warm.

To Assemble The Burrito: Lay a warm tortilla on a flat working surface. Place ¼ cup of rice down the center of the tortilla. Top the rice with ¾ cup of the cooked chicken pieces. Spoon ¼ cup of salsa over chicken. Top the salsa with a sprinkling of fresh spinach leaves (about ½ cup).

Makes 4 burritos

MANGO PESTO SALSA

Use this sauce for the Lahaina Sunset Burrito.

1 cup	ripe **mango,** diced
½ cup	sweet **Maui onion,** diced
½ cup	ripe **tomato,** diced
¼ cup	fresh squeezed **lime juice**
2 tablespoons	prepared **pesto sauce**

Mix all ingredients together. Serve immediately or keep in the refrigerator.

Makes about 2 cups.

GARLIC AHI BURRITO

*Fresh Ahi—a.k.a. yellowfin tuna—is the best fish for this
particular burrito, but you can use any kind of mild, firm fish you prefer.
The fish is quickly "seared" so it's well-done on the outside
and very rare in the middle . . . a classic Chef Ellman preparation.*

4	pesto or flour **tortillas** (10–12-inch size)
1 cup	**cabbage,** sliced very thin and chilled in ice water
1/2 cup	Dijon **mustard**
1/2 cup	**mayonnaise**
	bottled **hot sauce,** any kind
1	**cucumber,** long thin slices peeled
1 pound	fresh **ahi** or firm fish, diced into 1/2 inch cubes
1/4 cup	sliced **garlic cloves**
1	fresh **lemon,** juiced
1/4 cup	**olive oil**
1/4 cup	fresh **cilantro,** chopped
1 tablespoon	**furikake flakes**
	salt and **pepper** to taste

Drain excess water from the sliced cabbage. Mix cabbage with mayonnaise and mustard. Season to taste with salt and pepper. Add two shots of hot sauce and mix again.

Peel the cucumber. Cut the cucumber lengthwise into long paper-thin slices about 1″ wide.

Warm the tortillas. Cover them with foil (to keep them warm) and work with one at a time.

Sauté the fish cubes in a very hot frying pan with olive oil for one minute. Add garlic, salt and pepper. Cook for one more minute and add lemon juice.

In each warm tortilla, place a bed of cabbage mixture, then the ahi. Top with some of the cucumber slices. Sprinkle with cilantro and furikake flakes.

Wrap the tortilla in foil or serve on a warmed plate.

Makes 4 burritos

Chef's tip: What's furikake flakes? This seasoned seaweed mix is found in the Oriental food section in most stores. It is often vacuum-packed in a small glass jar or in a plastic bag. It usually has sesame seeds and other spices in the mix. The flakes are the secret ingredient in lots of fish preparations in upscale Hawaii restaurants.

MAUI-MEX-CHINESE CHICKEN WRAP

Hoisin sauce and Pineapple Salsa . . . together at last! This unlikely combination of salty, sweet and spicy gives your mouth a most pleasant surprise. These savory "wraps" are simple enough for a quick lunch . . . or simply delightful as a main dish for dinner guests. This recipe is a great way to use left over chicken, too.

4	flour **tortillas** (10–12 inch size)
8 tablespoons	**hoisin sauce**
1 ounce	**sesame seeds,** toasted
¼ cup	**green onions,** minced
2 cups	shredded cooked **chicken***
2 cups	shredded **lettuce**
1 cup	**pineapple salsa** (see page 25)

Warm the tortillas. Cover with foil (to keep them warm) and work with them one at a time.

Spread two tablespoons of Hoisin sauce on each tortilla, and then sprinkle with toasted sesame seeds and minced green onions. Use ¼ of the shredded chicken meat per tortilla, placing it on top of the Hoisin sauce.

Top chicken with shredded lettuce. Ladle pineapple salsa on top of lettuce.

Roll each tortilla as shown in the Burrito Folding section. Wrap in precut foil squares for casual dining.

Makes 4 burritos

*Save time. Use left-over chicken . . . or buy a deli counter rotisserie chicken. Shred the chicken into bite size pieces.

MAUI-MEX-CALIFORNIA ROLL BURRITO

(The Original and Still The Best)

Use several "colors" and flavors of tortillas to create an attractive buffet of these irresistible Maui-Mex California Rolls.

For each California Roll use:

1	flour **tortilla** (any flavor or color, 10–12 inch size)
1 sheet	**nori** (toasted seaweed sheets used for sushi)
¼ cup	**jasmine rice**
¼ cup	cooked **crabmeat** (King or Dungeness)
¼	large **avocado,** sliced into thin wedges
1 teaspoon	**pickled ginger,** finely chopped
1 teaspoon	toasted **sesame seeds**

The recipe makes ONE roll. Multiply ingredients by the number of rolls needed. Warm the tortillas. Cover them with foil and keep warm. Work with one tortilla a time.

Place a warm tortilla on a sheet of waxed paper on a flat surface. Lay one sheet of nori on top of the tortilla. Top the nori with a long mound of Jasmine rice right down the center.

Top the rice with a line of crabmeat (free of any shells or cartilage). Add the avocado slices alongside the line of crabmeat. Sprinkle with chopped pickled ginger and sesame seeds.

Use the waxed paper under the tortilla to help roll it all into a "tube" about 2″ in diameter. Chill rolls for easier slicing and especially if they will not be served right away. Slice rolls into 1″ slices and serve with soy sauce (shoyu) and Wasabi.

Serving suggestion:

- Go for lots of color with these. Use spinach, red pepper and flour tortillas. The flavor of these tortillas is subtle, so it doesn't overpower the roll.
- Serve the sliced rolls on a bed of finely shredded Napa cabbage on an attractive plate.
- Use a small mound of pickled ginger for a colorful bright pink garnish.
- Offer chopsticks (or tell everyone to pick up the sushi with their fingers.)

THE MAUI-MEX-GREEK FETA WRAP

You don't even need a fork to eat this fresh and crispy
Greek salad all rolled up in a warm tortilla.

4	flour **tortillas,** 10–12 inch (tomato, spinach or garlic flavor)
2 cups	shredded **lettuce**
¾ cup	**salsa,** any style
4 ounces	crumbled **feta cheese**
1 cup	**tomatoes,** diced
½ cup	**red onion,** thinly sliced
10	Greek **kalamata olives,** pitted and sliced
2 cups	shredded cooked **chicken**
1 cup	hot cooked **rice**

Heat the tortillas. Cover them with foil (to keep them warm) and work with one at a time.

Place ¼ of the lettuce and salsa on each tortilla. Sprinkle ¼ of the crumbled feta, tomato, red onion and sliced kalamata olives on the lettuce.

Use ¼ of the shredded chicken meat and rice per tortilla, placing it on top of the lettuce.

Roll each tortilla as a burrito. Wrap in foil, if desired.

Makes 4

THE ALL AMERICAN BBQ WRAP

Kids will love this wrap with ground beef, but you can substitute shredded chicken or left-over steak. Add a salad and you've made dinner.

4	flour **tortillas** (10–12 inch)
1 pound	**ground beef,** cooked and crumbled
1 cup	**BBQ sauce,** any flavor
2 cups	Maui-Mex **pinto beans** (see page 3)
2 cups	sharp **cheddar cheese,** shredded
1/2 cup	**cilantro,** chopped
1/2 cup	**onion,** chopped

Cook the ground beef in a frying pan, draining off any fat. Keep cooked meat warm. Heat the tortillas. Cover them with foil to keep them warm and work with one at a time.

Assemble each burrito: Put 1/4 of the cooked ground beef on a tortilla and top with BBQ sauce (to taste). Spoon on 1/4 of the pinto beans. Top with some of the shredded cheese, cilantro and diced onion.

Roll each tortilla as a burrito. Wrap in foil and serve.

Makes 4 wraps

KULA ROASTED VEGGIE BREAKFAST BURRITO

Save time by roasting the veggies the night before. Reheat them while cooking the eggs in the morning. Wrap it all up in a piece of foil and head for the beach. They say this burrito will sustain the average surfer for a full morning of action down at Big Beach in Makena.

¹/₂ cup	**Maui onion,** sliced
¹/₂ cup	**potato,** diced into ¹/₄ inch pieces
¹/₂ cup	**Japanese eggplant,** diced into ¹/₄ inch pieces
8 pieces	**red pepper strips,** ¹/₄ inch wide
¹/₂ cup	**shiitake mushrooms,** sliced
¹/₄ cup	**macadamia nut oil**
2 teaspoons	**Hawaiian** or **kosher salt** (kiawe-smoked is best)
2 teaspoons	fresh ground **black pepper**
1	**lemon,** juice only
	hot sauce (Hula Heat is good)
8	**egg whites**
1 tablespoon	minced **chives**
1 tablespoon	minced **parsley**
pinch	ground **nutmeg** (or to taste)
4	flour **tortillas,** any style, 12 inch
¹/₂ cup	shredded **cheddar cheese**

On a non-stick sheet pan, arrange the Maui Onion, potato, Japanese eggplant, red pepper and shittake mushrooms. Using a pastry brush, coat the veggies with a mixture of macadamia nut oil, Hawaiian salt, lemon juice and pepper.

Place the tray of coated veggies in a 375 degree oven for 30 to 45 minutes. Roast the veggies until evenly cooked and slightly browned. Remove from oven. Sprinkle hot sauce on the veggies. Mix to coat.

Meanwhile, whisk egg whites for 30 seconds in a bowl. Whisk in minced chives, parsley and nutmeg. Slowly cook the egg whites (until firm) over medium heat in a non-stick coated omelet pan. Remove the cooked egg and julienne into ¹/₂ inch strips.

To assemble the Breakfast Burritos: Heat the tortillas, one at a time, in the omelet pan or skillet. Spoon half of the veggies and half of the eggs in the center of each warm tortilla. Top them with shredded cheddar cheese. Wrap the filled tortillas burrito-style and serve.

Makes 4 burritos

Note: Instead of using a pastry brush to coat the veggies, try putting them and the mac-nut oil mixture in a tightly closed plastic bag. Shake to evenly coat the veggies.

Free "Shaka" with every meal

HAIKU POTATO AND EGG BREAKFAST BURRITO

A variation on the Haiku Vegetarian Burrito, this burrito is a
"Breakfast in a Tortilla." For the meat eaters at the table,
feel free to add some cooked breakfast sausage or bacon.

4	flour **tortillas,** 12-inch (any flavor)
2 cups	cooked Maui-Mex **potatoes**
6	**eggs**
¾ cup	shredded **cheddar cheese**
	salsa to taste

Warm the tortillas. Cover with foil (to keep them warm) and work with them one at a time.

Cook the potatoes according to the Maui-Mex Potato recipe on page 12. Divide the cooked potatoes between the warm tortillas.

Mix the eggs with two teaspoons of water and scramble softly in the pan used to cook the potatoes.

Layer the eggs and cheese over the potato in the warm tortillas.

Roll tortillas up like a burrito. Serve with biscuits and sliced fresh fruit.

Makes 4 burritos

Chef's tip—Burritos on the Side: The Haiku Potato burrito makes an unusual side dish for dinner. Take a break from baked potatoes. Roll up a bunch of these burritos and refrigerate or freeze them in individual freezer bags. Remove them from the freezer bags, wrap loosely in a paper towel and reheat them in the microwave. They can also be reheated in the oven along with almost any entrée.

One burrito can provide two servings when eaten as a side dish.

TOWERING HUEVOS RANCHEROS NAPOLEON

This is an excellent brunch dish. The presentation borders on elegant, but these eggs are hearty enough to serve to hungry surfers after an early morning at the beach.

Ingredients per serving:		
	1	**corn tortilla** (six-inch)
		vegetable or corn **oil** for frying tortilla
	2	**eggs**
	¼ cup	**pinto beans**
	¼ cup	**Spanish rice** (recipe page 8)
	¼ cup	**enchilada sauce** (recipe page 19)
	¼ cup	shredded **cheddar cheese**
	1 tablespoon	**sour cream**
	1 tablespoon	**guacamole** (recipe page 36)
	1 teaspoon	minced fresh **cilantro**
		salt to taste

Add a thin coating of vegetable oil to a medium size frying pan. Fry the tortilla(s) until golden brown, but not too crisp. Remove to paper towel. Lightly sprinkle with salt while it is still warm.

Cook the eggs "over easy" in the same frying pan after draining excess oil. Remove, set aside and keep warm.

To assemble: For each serving, scoop rice and beans onto an oven-proof plate. Place the fried tortilla on top.

Arrange the cooked eggs on top of the tortilla. Drizzle enchilada sauce over the eggs and top with shredded cheese.

Place the plate in the oven under the broiler element (set on medium) just until the cheese is melted. Remove from oven and top with sour cream and guacamole. Sprinkle with minced cilantro.

THE PORTUGUESE SUPER MAN BREAKFAST BURRITO

with Grilled Pineapple

This recipe combines traditional Hawaiian taro with the favorite breakfast meat on Maui—spicy Portuguese sausage. Mark prefers purple taro (known locally as Lehua) and low acid pineapple (labeled as Hawaiian Gold) for the best results with this recipe.

1 cup	Portuguese sausage
1 cup	cooked **taro** or potato, diced (¼ inch)
2 tablespoons	**butter**
4	extra large **eggs**
1 tablespoon	**water**
2 tablespoons	minced **green onions**
4 slices	**pineapple,** sliced ¼ inch thick.
4	flour **tortillas,** burrito size any flavor (optional)
	sour cream and **Hula Heat** Hot Sauce to taste

Cook the sausage in a non-stick sauté pan. Drain and slice the sausage into thin rings or strips about ¼ inch wide by 1 inch long.

Return sausage to pan with the cooked taro (or potato) and butter. Over medium heat, cook for 2 minutes.

Mix the eggs with a tablespoon of water. Add eggs and green onion to the pan and cook until desired consistency.

Sear pineapple slices over an open flame or in a grilling pan until caramelized on both sides. Dice the pineapple into ¼ inch pieces.

Place cooked eggs on serving plate or wrap as a burrito. Garnish with a tablespoon of sour cream and some Hawaiian Hula Hot Sauce. Sprinkle the eggs with warm pineapple.

Makes 4 burritos

THE HAWAIIAN
BREAKFAST WRAP

It's fairly easy to find taro root and fiddlehead fern in Hawaii,
but a regular potato (or sweet potato) and asparagus tips work fine in this recipe.
It's still surprisingly different for breakfast . . . and a real eye-opener
if you use as much chili water as Chef Mark!

4	spinach **tortillas** (10–12 inch size)
2 cups	cooked **taro** (substitute: **potato** or **sweet potato**)
3 cups	fiddlehead fern shoots (or **asparagus tips**)
	salsa of your choice, to taste
1 cup	**jalapeño jack cheese,** grated
6 large	**eggs,** scrambled softly

Peel and cut the taro root (or potato) into 1″ cubes. Cook the pieces in gently boiling water until they are soft. Mash while still warm, but leave potatoes a bit chunky.

Blanch fresh fiddlehead ferns (or asparagus tips) in boiling water just until crisp-tender. Chop into ¹/₂ inch pieces.

Mix the salsa and shredded cheese.

Scramble the eggs and keep warm.

Warm the tortillas. Cover them with foil (to keep them warm) and work with one tortilla at a time.

Use ¹/₄ of each prepared ingredient per tortilla and assemble in this order: Tortilla, cheese/salsa mixture, taro/potato mixture, eggs, and finally the fern/asparagus.

Roll up each tortilla like a burrito. Wrap in foil and serve.

Makes 4 burritos

MAUI-MEX ITEMS RIGHT OFF THE MENU

Here it is . . . the Maui Tacos taco! This chapter includes tacos and all the other entree items that are regulars on the menu.

THE MAUI TACOS
SOFT TACO

Tacos were invented to transport meat from the plate to the mouth . . .
without the use of fork, knife and spoon. How beautifully efficient is that?
Burritos may be the biggest seller at Maui Tacos, but you've got to try the tacos!

These soft tacos require TWO corn tortillas to keep all the fillings
from falling in your lap. The inner tortilla soaks up the juices of the fillings,
while the outer tortilla is a back-up. It holds the taco together.
The result is a substantial and chewy taco.

For EACH taco:	2	corn **tortillas,** 6 inch*
	2 ounces	cooked **chicken** or **steak**
	1 ounce	shredded iceberg **lettuce**
	1 ounce	shredded **cheese**
		(cheddar, Monterey jack, etc.)
		assorted salsas and/or condiments to taste

Heat a griddle or Teflon coated sauté pan to medium. Lay a tortilla directly on the surface and it will "steam" cook, using the natural moisture in the tortilla. Flip the tortilla over when the top feels soft and pliable. Steam the tortilla for 5 to 7 seconds per side.

Stack the warm tortillas on a plate and cover them with a cloth napkin to keep them warm.

To build the taco: Gently bend and hold two warm tortillas, one on top of the other, in your hand or in a taco rack. Place the cooked chicken or steak (or other desired filling . . . such as carnitas or beans) in the taco shell. Top with shredded lettuce and cheese.

Customize each taco with condiments from your "home version" salsa bar. See Chapter 2

*Use two corn tortillas to keep the taco from tearing. If using flour tortillas, use just one tortilla.

ISLAND FISH TACOS

Maybe it was the name "Fish Taco" that people had a hard time accepting. Once they tasted it, though, they were hooked . . .

³/₄ pound	**ahi** or firm white fish, cleaned and ready to cook
¹/₄ cup	**olive oil**
¹/₂	fresh **lime,** juice only
¹/₂ teaspoon	granulated **garlic**
¹/₂ teaspoon	**oregano** leaves
	salt and **pepper** to taste
8	corn **tortillas,** 6 inch
1 cup	shredded iceberg **lettuce** (or shredded cabbage)
	assorted **salsas** and/or condiments to taste

Marinate the fish with olive oil, lime juice, garlic and oregano about an hour before cooking.

Warm the tortillas and wrap them until ready to use. Grill the fish or sauté it quickly in a non-stick pan over medium high heat. Use the marinade to baste the fish but don't add so much it "boils" the fish. You want a nice firm and ever so slightly browned chunk of fish. Add salt and pepper to taste. Break the cooked fish into bite size chunks making sure to remove any bones or skin.

Use two tortillas per taco. Fill the four tacos with an equal amount of cooked fish and top with some lettuce. Be sure to finish with the drippings in the pan as a sauce over the fish and lettuce.

Serve warm, just as it is, or finish with your favorite salsa and condiments from Chapter 2.

Makes four tacos

HARD TACOS

Hard or soft . . . It is purely personal preference when it comes to tacos.
The fillings are the same, but only one corn tortilla is required per hard taco.

For EACH taco:

	corn **tortilla,** 6 inch
2 ounces	cooked **chicken** or **steak**
1 ounce	shredded iceberg **lettuce**
1 ounce	shredded **cheese**
	(cheddar, Monterey jack, etc.)
	assorted condiments to taste (see below)

Heat ¾ of an inch of vegetable oil to 350 degrees in a frying pan.

Using tongs, gently place a corn tortilla into the oil. The tortilla will soften in a few seconds.

Before it gets crisp, fold the tortilla while it is still in the hot oil. Try to form a half circle . . . but not exactly in half. The top edges of the tortilla should be 1 to 2 inches apart. This is the best shape for a taco shell.

Continue to fry the tortilla until the underside is crispy, then turn the tortilla over with the tongs to fry the other side until equally crispy. Do not let the tortilla turn brown.

Drain the fried tortilla on a dry paper towel and let it cool slightly. Set each finished hard taco shell in a taco shell holder . . . or hold it in your hand so it is easy to fill.

Now, create the perfect taco! Place some cooked chicken or steak (or other desired filling . . . such as carnitas or beans) in the taco shell. Top with shredded lettuce and cheese.

Customize each taco with condiments from your home version salsa bar. See The Salsa Bar Chapter for suggestions.

MARK'S FAVORITE POTATO TAQUITOS

"These are my absolute favorite taquito," says Mark.
The potato filled tortillas are rolled and lightly deep fried.
Serve with Avocado Salsa and sour cream

1¹/₂ cup	**Maui Tacos Potatoes** (see recipe page 12)
12	6 inch **corn tortillas** at room temperature
24	**wood toothpicks**
	vegetable oil
Garnish:	**Avocado Salsa** (see page 29)
	sour cream and chopped **cilantro**

If the tortillas are not pliable, warm them. The easiest way is to wrap them in a paper towel and microwave them for 30 seconds.

Place a tortilla flat on a table. Place 2 tablespoons of potato down the center staying ¹/₂ inch from the ends of the tortilla. Gently roll the tortilla up (not too tight) but firm enough so the filling does not fall out. Use a toothpick at the top and bottom of the rolled tortilla to hold it together. Stack on a platter.

Heat an inch of vegetable oil to 350 degrees in a shallow frying pan. Gently place a few of the taquitos into the oil. Don't overcrowd the pan. Fry for 2 to 3 minutes or until the tortilla is crispy. Drain taquitos on paper towels. Repeat with all of the taquitos.

Serve taquitos with sour cream and Avocado Salsa in separate ramekins. Sprinkle as much fresh chopped cilantro on salsa and sour cream as you like. Serve immediately.

Makes 12

AWESOME BAKED NACHOS

Who doesn't know that nachos are an excellent snack?
A few chips, some cheese, a minute in a microwave . . . So easy, brah!

But nachos can be transformed into a satisfying meal and they taste
even better when baked to crispy perfection. Use the recipe below, then
pile on some shredded meat or chicken, grilled fresh veggies or black beans.

If you want to transcend the ordinary, top your nachos with grilled
shrimp and mango salsa for Maui-Mex at its best.

5 cups	fresh **tortilla chips**
1 1/2 cups	grated **cheddar cheese***
1/3 cup	**guacamole**
1/3 cup	**sour cream**
1 cup	fresh diced **tomatoes**
1/4 cup	fresh chopped **cilantro**
	sliced **jalapeños** to taste

Heat oven to 325 degrees. Arrange cooked tortilla chips evenly in a 10 inch pie pan or ovenproof plate. Sprinkle with grated cheese. Bake for 7 minutes or until cheese is completely melted.

Remove plate from oven. Spoon the guacamole and sour cream side by side in the center of the chips. Sprinkle with diced tomatoes, cilantro, and as many sliced jalapeños as you can stand.

For variety, try topping nachos with:

- Cooked chicken, steak, ground beef, turkey,
- Crumbled chorizo or linguica sausage, diced duck . . .
- Black beans or refried pinto beans . . .
- Fresh grilled fish or sautéd scallops . . .
- Grilled shrimp and mango salsa.

Serves 4

*Cheese . . . the perfect one is a personal thing. Experiment with different cheeses (goat, brie, jalapeño cheese) and compliment the nachos with different salsas.

FLAT IS BEAUTIFUL
BEAN TOSTADA

A tostada is built on a flat, crispy, tortilla. Mark says one of his favorite meals at home is a simple "make your own" tostada. "We lay out a good selection of ingredients and everyone helps themselves to their favorite toppings." Simple enough . . .

	vegetable oil for frying
4	**corn tortillas,** any size
1 cup	**refried beans**
1¹⁄₂ cup	shredded **romaine lettuce**
1 cup	**queso fresco** or other shredded **cheese**
¹⁄₂ cup	**sour cream**
¹⁄₂ cup	**guacamole** or a peeled, sliced **avocado**
	Pico de Gallo salsa or **hot sauce,** to taste

Heat oil in frying pan to 350 degrees. Fry the tortillas until flat and crispy. Drain on paper towels on a platter.

In the following order, place ¹⁄₄ of each ingredient on top of the tostada shell: beans, shredded lettuce and cheese.

Top with guacamole, sour cream and salsa.

KITCHEN SINK TOSTADA

For a Chicken, Steak, Potato, Fish or Ground Beef Tostada: Prepare tostada as above but top the beans with ¹⁄₄ cup or more of the selected ingredient(s).

Makes 4 tostadas

SO SIMPLE NO-BAKE ENCHILADAS

We considered it, but you can't bake an enchilada in an imu oven.
Rather than heat up the kitchen, this version of the classic
baked entree is zapped in a microwave.

4	**corn tortillas** (large size)
2 1/2 cups	grated **cheddar cheese**
1 cup	**enchilada sauce** (page 19)

Have a 9″ × 9″ glass (or microwaveable) baking dish ready. Soften the tortillas . . . wrap them in a paper towel or clean dish cloth and microwave for 30 seconds.

Place one tortilla at a time on a flat surface. Place 1/2 cup of cheese in the tortilla. Roll so the flaps are on the bottom and place in the baking dish. Repeat and line up the tortillas so they hold each other from unrolling. Sprinkle with half of the remaining cheese.

Ladle enchilada sauce on top of the rolled tortillas, covering them completely with sauce. Sprinkle the remaining cheese on top.

Immediately place in microwave and heat until the cheese inside is melted.

CHICKEN, STEAK, GROUND BEEF OR FISH ENCHILADAS

Add to the cheese in the tortillas: 1 cup of cooked shredded chicken, sliced steak, crumbled ground beef or sautéd fish. Prepare as above.

POTATO ENCHILADAS

Replace the cheese in the tortillas—or add to it—with 1/3 cup of Maui-Mex potato in each tortilla. Prepare as above, but top with the pan of enchiladas with Green Tomatillo sauce instead of the red enchilada sauce.

Serve with a side boat of rice and beans.

"WAS IT A DREAM?" MUSHROOM QUESADILLAS

*I got off a plane at the Mexico City airport. The first thing I looked for
was a food stand where I could taste authentic street food.
I stopped at the first stand I saw, and it was a lasting memory.*

Mushroom filling:	1 1/3 tablespoons	**unsalted butter**
	2 tablespoons	**olive oil,** divided
	2 cups	sliced **mushrooms**
	2 cloves	chopped **garlic**
	1 tablespoon	fresh **lemon juice**
	1/4 cup	fresh chopped **cilantro**
	8	thin slices of **jack cheese**
	8	**corn** or **flour tortillas** (6 inch)

Heat the unsalted butter and one tablespoon of olive oil in a sauté pan. When the butter is melted, add the sliced mushrooms and chopped garlic. Sauté for three minutes until well cooked. Drizzle with lemon juice and sprinkle with fresh chopped cilantro. Cool.

In a Teflon pan, add remaining olive oil and heat over medium heat. Heat a corn tortilla, top with a quarter of the mushroom mixture and two slices of cheese. Top with another tortilla.

Continue to heat and when the cheese melts, flip it to cook on both sides. Continue to cook until slightly crispy and the cheese is melted.

Serve immediately with your favorite hot sauce . . .

Makes 4

MAUI-MEX EXTRA SPECIAL ENTREES

Always, and we mean always, check the "specials board"
at a Maui Tacos. When Chef Pepe and Chef Sergio
are inspired by something fresh and flavorful at the market,
there's no telling what wonderful recipe they will cook up.
Here are just a few of their favorite entrées.

CHEF PEPE'S SPECIAL CARNITAS

Huge frozen pork butts are a staple in Hawaiian markets.
Most are transformed into kalua pig, but Chef Pepe uses them in this recipe.
Cuts of pork without bone or excess fat will have more usable meat,
so adjust the rest of the seasonings.

Carnitas is a tender pork dish that's full of flavor.
Searing the meat keeps the it juicy and slightly crusty
with a hint of citrus and cumin. Pepe even reveals his secret
ingredient—Coca Cola®!

5 pound	frozen **pork butt** (defrosted)
	vegetable shortening
1 teaspoon	ground **cumin**
1	**bay leaf**
1 tablespoon	Hawaiian or regular **salt**
¹/₂ cup	**orange juice**
¹/₂ can	**cola soda**

Trim pork butt of bones and excess fat. Cut pork in 3″ cubes. Add shortening to a large pot or Dutch oven to a depth of ¹/₂ inch. Heat the shortening on high heat. When oil is very hot, but not smoking, add the meat cubes. Toss and sear the meat on all sides.

Reduce heat and continue cooking for 10 minutes. Drain excess oil but leave all crusty bits of pork in the pot with the meat.

Add salt, cumin and bay leaf to the pot with the meat. Stir until meat is coated and golden brown.

Lower heat to medium and pour orange juice over the meat. Simmer until tender—the longer the better. Stir every few minutes until the meat is tender but still juicy. Just before meat is ready to be removed from the pot, add just enough of the soda to the pan to coat the meat (may be less than half the can). Simmer until the soda and orange juice have turned into a rich glaze on the meat. Remove the carnitas meat from the pot with a slotted spoon.

Serve as an entrée with the sauce that follows . . . or roll the meat up in a tortilla either taco or burrito style.

Serves 4 as an entrée

SAUCE FOR CARNITAS

2 cloves	**garlic**
¼ cup	**water**
¼ cup	**white vinegar**
⅛ cup	**jalapeño juice**
	(reserved from canned chiles)
3	whole **tomatoes**
10	whole **tomatillos**
¼ cup	pickled **jalapeño,**
	"en escabeche" style in can
¼ teaspoon	**oregano**
1	**onion,** diced
	salt to taste

In a blender, combine garlic with water, vinegar and jalapeño juice. Blend to a very smooth liquid.

Cut tomatoes and tomatillos into small chunks and add them to the blender. Add the jalapeño en escabeche. Pulse ingredients in blender to a chunky consistency.

Add diced onion and oregano. Salt to taste.

GRILLED RED SNAPPER IN TEQUILA-ORANGE MARINADE

*Cook this marinated snapper over deliciously smoky mesquite coals
on an outdoor grill for the best possible flavor. Then serve this fresh fish entrée
at a backyard get-together or sunset beach party . . .*

*Don't forget the icy Margaritas because technically, the tequila in the marinade
will be rendered non-alcoholic after the grilling!*

1 cup	**orange juice**
1	smoked **chipotle chile** in adobo
¼ cup	melted unsalted **butter**
2 cloves	finely chopped **garlic**
3 tablespoons	chopped **cilantro**
¼ cup	**tequila**
1 teaspoon	**salt**
1 whole	fresh **red snapper,** cleaned and butterflied.

In a blender, combine the orange juice and chipotle in adobo. Blend until smooth.

Pour mixture into a bowl. Add melted butter, chopped garlic, salt, cilantro and tequila. Mix well.

With a basting brush, generously coat the whole fish with this marinade at least one hour before grilling. Keep some marinade for basting while the fish is cooking later. Keep fish refrigerated.

To grill: Start the fire with kiawe or mesquite wood or charcoal. The coals should be hot and have a white ash on them. Make a bed of aluminum foil on the grill rack. The outer edges of the foil should be rolled and raised up about ¼ inch to keep marinade from dripping on coals.

Place the whole split fish down on the foil, with skin up. Brush on more marinade. Cook for 4–6 minutes; then turn the fish over. (For added flavor at this point, you can remove the foil. The skin of the fish should keep the fish from falling through the grill (but no money back guarantees, brah!)

Brush on more marinade and continue to grill the fish until it is white all the way through.

Or not to grill: The marinated fish can be cooked in a hot oven (350 degrees) using a baking pan instead of the foil. Use the same preparation, marinating and cooking method as above except for removing the fish from the pan during cooking!

Serve with rice and salsa. Chef Pepe suggests Arroz Con Rajas De Chile Poblano (page 10 and Mango Pineapple Salsa (page 27).

Serves 4

SHAMELESSLY NAKED CHILE RELLENO...

Chef Pepe makes a stuffed chile that is delightfully different and much lighter than the batter dipped version. Cotija cheese is the best choice for the filling, but you can substitute a soft, mild cheese if it isn't available.

4	**chile poblanos** (roasted, seeded and peeled)
1 cup	fresh **corn kernels**
1 cup	**cotija cheese**
	(substitute jack or other mild cheese)
2 tablespoons	chopped **cilantro**
2 tablespoons	chopped **basil**
1 cup	**salsa** (Hola Aloha suggested)
	salt to taste

Roast chiles under a broiler or directly over a flame until the skin is charred. Let chiles cool in a paper bag for a few minutes, then slip the peel off the chiles. Slit each chile carefully down one side and remove the seeds. Leave the stem on the chile for presenation.

In a medium bowl mix the corn, cheese, cilantro and basil. Stuff the chiles with the mix.

Preheat the oven to 350 degrees. Arrange the chiles in a lightly greased baking dish. Bake the chiles until the cheese is melted . . . about 15 minutes.

Cover the chiles with warm salsa. Serve with beans and rice.

Makes 4

OLD MEXICO STYLE STEAK WITH ONIONS

According to Chef Sergio, steak with onions (or Bisteces Encebollados)
is an extremely popular entrée in small restaurants in Mexico.
In these fondas, the chef often substitutes beer for the water in the recipe.
A good Mexican beer goes great with this entrée after it's cooked, too!

2 pounds	boneless beef, **sirloin, filet,** or **New York**
	salt and freshly ground **pepper** to taste
¼ cup	vegetable **oil**
3 large	sliced **onions**
3 cloves	**garlic,** minced
½ cup	**water** or **beer**

Trim away excess fat from the steak(s) and season with salt and pepper. Heat three tablespoons of the oil in a large skillet. Sauté the meat over medium-high heat for 1 or 2 minutes on each side. Transfer to a platter and cut steak into strips 1 inch thick. Set the platter of meat aside.

Add the remaining tablespoon of oil to the skillet. Sauté the onions and garlic until they are golden brown. Add the strips of steak and any juices on the platter. Add the water (or beer).

Adjust seasonings and cook, covered, over low heat for 5 minutes. If too much liquid cooks off, add a bit of water or beer.

Serves 4 generously

SMOKIN' CHICKEN
WITH CHILES

This is traditionally a spicy stew, but Pollo Al Chipotle
*can be as hot or mild as you like. Chef Sergio uses three chipotle chiles
to balance the smoky flavor and spicy heat.*

*It's perfectly okay to use frozen chicken thighs or any other part
of the chicken you prefer.*

3 pounds	boneless, skinless **chicken thighs and legs**
	salt and freshly ground **pepper**
1/2 cup	**water,** divided
3 cloves	**garlic**
4 whole	**black peppercorns**
2 whole	**cloves**
1/2 teaspoon	ground **cumin**
1/4	small **onion**
2 tablespoons	**vegetable oil**
2	medium **onions,** sliced
5	small **tomatoes,** thinly sliced
3	canned **chipotle chiles**

Season the chicken with salt and pepper. Set aside.

In a blender, add 1/4 cup water and make a puree of the garlic, peppercorns, cloves, cumin and onion. Keep the blender handy . . .

Heat the oil in a large skillet to medium-high. Cook the sliced onions until transparent. Stir in the puree and continue to cook for 10 minutes. Add the tomatoes and bring to a boil. Lower the heat, cover the skillet and cook for 5 minutes.

Puree the remaining water and chiles in the blender. Add to the mixture in the skillet and boil for 2 minutes. Add the chicken pieces, recover the skillet and cook for 25 minutes or until the chicken is tender.

Serves 4

CHICKEN IN
MAC NUT SAUCE

Macadamia nuts are a favorite ingredient for Hawaiian cooks.
Here is the very traditional "Chicken in Nut Sauce" entrée done up Maui-Mex style.
Usually peanuts would be used in the sauce, but since this is a mild version
(no chiles) the subtle Mac nut flavor isn't lost.

¼ cup	**vegetable oil**
1	cut up **chicken** (about 3 pounds)
2 cups	**chicken stock**
1	**onion** cut into chunks
1 clove	**garlic,** chopped
1	**cinnamon stick** (1″ long)
2 whole	**allspice**
3	**tomatoes**
½ cup	chopped **macadamia nuts**
½ cup	**dry sherry**
	salt to taste

Cut up the chicken into serving size pieces. Heat oil in skillet to medium high. Sauté chicken pieces until nicely browned. Transfer the chicken to a large pot. Cover with chicken stock and cook until the chicken pieces are tender (about 30 minutes). When done, pour off the stock into a large measuring cup. Leave the chicken in the pot.

Sauté the onion chunks, garlic, cinnamon and allspice in the chicken drippings in the skillet. Remove the sautéed ingredients with a slotted spoon (to drain the oil) and put them in the blender. Peel, seed and chop the tomatoes. Add them to the blender along with the macadamia nuts, and ½ cup of stock from the chicken pot. Blend until the sauce is very smooth. Add the sherry to the sauce.

Pour the sauce over the chicken in the pot. Cover the pot and cook over low heat until the sauce thickens. Add salt to taste.

Serves 4 generously

SAVOR THESE SHRIMP

(Shrimp in the Style of Tamaulipas)

*This recipe is a seaside café classic. It yields a bouillabaisse-like sauce
and works well with any size shrimp. It is quick and easy,
but tastes like an elegant entrée.*

3 tablespoons	vegetable or **olive oil**
1 small	**Maui onion,** chopped
2 cloves	**garlic,** chopped
2	large ripe **tomatoes,** chopped
1	**bay leaf**
1 pound	**shrimp,** peeled and deveined
	fresh ground **pepper** and **salt** to taste
	fresh **jalapeño pepper,** chopped (optional)
4 tablespoons	**butter**
2 tablespoons	fresh chopped **cilantro**

Heat oil in a saucepan over medium heat. Add onion and garlic to the pan and sauté for 30 seconds. Add tomato, bay leaf and shrimp. Season with pepper, salt and chili to taste. Cook over medium heat for 3 to 4 minutes or until the shrimp are just cooked. Add butter to the pan and lightly toss all the ingredients. Sprinkle with cilantro and remove from heat.

Serve with rice or over pasta.

Serves 4

MAUI-MEX SALADS AND SOUPS

Surprise! Guests are coming and you want to serve
more than a burrito wrapped in a sheet of aluminum foil.
So, how do we make a satisfying meal out of a simple burrito or taco?
Remove the foil . . . and add an interesting salad or
a homemade bowl of soup!

These recipes are full of attention-grabbing flavor.
In fact they make excellent entrées all by themselves—
especially for lunch or a light dinner meal.

SALADS

SOUPS

SIMPLE TACO SALAD
IN A SHELL

*Once you master making the tortilla shell that holds this salad,
you'll find the shells are a fun and impressive to serve a variety of items.
The "taco salad" ingredients listed below are only a suggestion.
Customize your salad with things you love to eat . . .*

4	**flour tortillas,** burrito size, any flavor
2 cups	**refried beans,** any kind
4 cups	shredded or torn **lettuce,** any kind
1 cup	shredded **cheese,** cheddar or jack
1/2 cup	**guacamole**
1/4 cup	**sour cream**
	large **tomato,** cut into wedges
1 pound	grilled **steak, ahi** or **chicken,** cut into strips

Poke the tortillas several times with a fork. These tiny holes in the tortilla let the air out so it will not bubble too much.

Preheat oven to 350 degrees. Place a 10 to 12 inch heat resistant bowl face down on cookie sheet. (If there is room, do two at a time.) Brush the bowl(s) with a thin light vegetable oil. Drape and shape the tortilla over the bowl. Place the entire tray and bowl(s) into the oven for about ten minutes. Check that the tortilla is crispy and a light golden brown. Remove the tortilla and repeat the process. Let tortillas cool for 5 minutes

Place the crispy tortilla on a plate that is dotted with a bit of smashed (refried) beans. This will hold the tortilla in place. In the bottom of the shell, place 1/4 cup of beans: black, pinto or smashed.

Top the beans with a cup of your favorite lettuce (or a mixture of lettuces). Sprinkle with grated cheese. Top with a dollop of guacamole and sour cream.

Lay wedges of fresh tomatoes on the salad and top with fresh grilled ahi, chicken or steak. Instead or in addition to the meat, add more of your favorite veggies (raw, cooked or grilled).

Some other ingredients to consider: Sliced olives, pickled jalapeño rings, avocado slices, strings of Maui onion, and diced mango. Use your favorite salsa as your dressing . . . Enjoy!

Serves 4

SEASIDE CEVICHE VIA TOSTADA

When we have access to really fresh fish or scallops, we think ceviche.
No need to be squeamish about raw fish. The pineapple and lime marinade will
"cook" the fish or scallops in this recipe. Mark likes to serve ceviche on fried tortilla—
like a tostada—to fully appreciate the complimentary texture and flavors.

1 pound	fresh deboned **snapper** fillet or **scallops** (or any white fish)
1 cup	fresh squeezed **lime juice**
½ cup	**pineapple juice**
1 cup	fresh diced **tomatoes**
1 cup	fresh diced **sweet onion**
¼ cup	fresh chopped **cilantro**
⅛ cup	canned **jalapeño juice**
	fresh **hot peppers** to taste, chopped
¼ cup	fresh **lime juice**
	salt and **pepper** and **hot sauce,** to taste
10	6″ **corn tortillas**
	vegetable oil for frying tortillas

Dice the seafood into ¼ inch cubes and marinate it in the lime and pineapple juice for four to six hours in the refrigerator.

Drain off the marinade. Add the rest of the ingredients except for the tortillas.

Mix and chill for one to two hours.

Fry the tortillas in ¼ inch of oil in a shallow frying pan just before serving the salad. They should be flat and crispy but not brown or their flavor will overpower the ceviche. Drain on paper towels.

Serve ceviche in a decorative bowl. Have the fried tortillas on a platter nearby. Spoon a thin layer of the cold ceviche on the tortillas to create a crispy tostada. Enjoy with a splash of your favorite hot sauce.

Serves 4 as a salad or appetizer

BAJA SHRIMP COCKTAIL GAZPACHO STYLE

Is this a recipe for a cold soup . . . or a salad? Either way, it is elegant to serve this shrimp cocktail in a chilled martini glass . . . perhaps with a rim of sea salt.

Why use large shrimp when they will be diced anyway? The texture of the cooked shrimp meat is firmer and holds its own with the chopped vegetables.

Shrimp and	24	medium to large **shrimp** in the shell
Stock:	6 cups	**water**
	1 cup	**white onion,** diced
	2 cups	fresh **tomato,** quartered
		salt and **pepper** to taste
	2	**cloves,** whole
	1 stalk	**celery,** diced

Bring water to a boil in a medium sized pot. Add all ingredients EXCEPT the shrimp. Boil for three minutes.

Add the shrimp and cook for 5 to 7 minutes. Remove shrimp with a slotted spoon and drop them into an ice bath to stop the cooking. Peel the shrimp and dice all but four of them into ½″ pieces. Place the shells of the shrimp into the stock in the pot. Continue cooking for 15 minutes. Strain and chill the stock.

Meanwhile peel,	1 cup	cucumber
seed and dice	1 cup	tomato
(into ¼ inch cubes):	1 cup	white **onion**
	1 cup	chopped **cilantro**

Toss the vegetables together gently. Chill this diced vegetable mixture and four cocktail or martini glasses.

Just before	1	small **avocado,** diced
serving:	¼ cup	**ketchup**
		Hula Heat to taste

Peel and dice the avocado into ½ inch cubes.

Using the chilled serving glasses, place ¼ of the diced shrimp into the bottom of each glass. Top with ½ cup of veggie mixture and 6 ounces of the chilled shrimp stock. Add ¼ of the diced avocado to each glass.

Mix the ketchup with Hula Heat Salsa to taste in a small bowl. Drizzle a bit on top of each cocktail. Stir gently and top with a whole shrimp thinly sliced and fanned out as a garnish.

Serve shrimp cocktails with wedges of lime and saltines on the side.

Makes 4 servings

PEPE'S "DESERT ISLAND" NOPALES SALAD

*Nopales—or paddle cactus—is available canned on the grocer's shelf
in the Mexican section. Ethnic markets often sell fresh, cleaned and cut up nopales.
So, Chef Pepe gives directions for working with it cooked or raw!*

"Serve this salad with carnitas," says Pepe.

4 cups	fresh **nopales** (or from can or jar, drained)
2 cloves	fresh **garlic**
1	**onion**
3	**tomatoes**
4	fresh green **jalapeños**
½ bunch	**cilantro**
1	**lime,** juice only
8 ounces	**feta cheese,** crumbled
	salt and **black pepper** to taste

If nopales are raw, clean off the thorns and dice the flesh into ½ inch cubes. Put in pot with fresh garlic and add water to cover. Bring to boil. Reduce heat and simmer until tender (about 5–7 minutes). Drain nopales and cool off with cold water to stop the cooking. For a quicker salad, just get diced canned nopales.

Dice the onion, tomatoes and jalapeños. Mix with drained nopales in a bowl. Add chopped cilantro, juice of the lime and feta cheese to the nopales. Mix well and add salt and pepper to taste. Makes an excellent side dish with pork entrees.

Serves 4

HEART WARMING POZOLE VERDE SOUP

*This soup is a meal in itself and great on a cold night.
On Maui that's when it gets below 70 degrees! Chef Pepe makes it simple
and uses canned hominy for this hearty soup. He always saves a tortilla
from the night before . . . just for this fabulous soup.*

1 pound	**pork butt**
8 cups	drained canned **hominy,** rinsed
3 cloves	**garlic**
2	serrano **chiles**
1/2 bunch	**cilantro,** tough stems removed
4	**romaine leaves**
10	**tomatillos,** husked and washed
1	whole **clove**
1 teaspoon	ground **cumin**
1	**tortilla** from the night before

Cut the pork into 2″ squares. Cover with water in a pot and bring to boil. Reduce the heat to medium. Cook the pork until tender.

Add the hominy to the pot. Roughly chop the garlic, serrano chiles, tortilla, cilantro, romaine and tomatillos. Add all of this along with the cumin and clove to the meat and hominy. Add a little water (if necessary) but try to retain a hearty soup consistency. Simmer for 10 minutes

Season as desired with the following condiments served in separate bowls at the table:

- shredded cabbage
- finely chopped white onions
- dried Mexican oregano
- finely chopped radishes
- Hola Aloha or Hula Heat hot salsa

Serves 4

TRADITIONAL TORTILLA SOUP

(SOPA de TORTILLA)

Chef Sergio shares his favorite recipe for a classic Mexican soup.
Add some shredded chicken, and it is a meal in a bowl!

This soup is made with lots of the ingredients most folks consider essential to
"Mexican" cooking. Epazote is a Mexican herb that has a unique taste . . .
sort of a pungent minty-oregano. The medium-hot pasillas chiles are
dried and purplish-black. If either are not available, cilantro and
other types of chiles can be substituted.

3 cloves	**garlic**
½	**onion,** cut into chunks
3	ripe **tomatoes**
6 cups	**chicken stock**
1 tablespoon	vegetable **oil**
2 sprigs	**epasote,** chopped
	salt and **pepper** to taste
8	stale **corn tortillas**
	(they are drier and fry better)
	vegetable **oil** for frying
2	**pasillas chiles**
2	**avocados,** peeled, pitted and sliced
5 ounces	**queso fresco** (or crumbled feta cheese)
½ cup	**cream fraiche***
3	**limes,** cut into wedges

Roast-toast the garlic, onion and tomatoes in a hot frying pan or under the broiler. The tomatoe skins will begin to "lift" off. Peel and core the tomatoes. Process the roasted tomatoes, onion and garlic in the blender with ¼ cup of chicken stock. Process until it is a tomato puree consistancy.

Heat a tablespoon of oil in a large saucepan over high heat. Saute the processed tomato puree in the pan. Let it boil for two minutes, then lower the heat. Cook, stirring constantly, for another five minutes or until the puree thickens and changes color.

Add remaining chicken stock and epasote. Return to a boil. Add salt and pepper to taste. Cover and cook over medium heat for 15 minutes. Up to this stage, the soup can be made ahead and refrigerated.

Prepare to serve: Cut stale tortillas in half, then into thin strips. Also, seed and chop the chilies into 1/2 inch rings.

Heat 1/2 inch of oil in a small skillet. First fry the tortilla strips in the hot oil until golden brown on both sides (3 minutes). Use slotted spoon to remove strips to a plate lined with paper towels. Fry chile rings in the same hot oil until crisp. Drain and set aside.

Five minutes before serving, reheat the soup. Add the fried tortilla strips. Garnish each bowl of soup with a few chile rings and some of the avocado. Sprinkle with crumbled cheese. Pass the cream fraiche, lime halves and chile rings and avocado in separate bowls.

Serves 4

*To finish this soup, Sergio adds a dollop of cream fraiche right at the table. To make it at home, combine 1/4 cup heavy cream and 1/4 cup buttermilk. Let it sit in the refriger-ator overnight to thicken.

TEMPTING TUNA BALL SOUP

Ahi Albondigas Soup

*This is an amazing soup to serve guests. Warm the bowls . . . and garnish
each serving with some freshly sautéed corn kernels,
cilantro and a drizzle of sour cream.*

1 pound	fresh **ahi,** (sashimi grade tuna)
2	**shallots,** chopped fine
1 tablespoon	fresh chopped **cilantro**
2	**egg yolks**
¼ teaspoon	**lemon zest**
	fresh chopped **chile pepper,** to taste
	salt and **pepper,** to taste
	panko flakes, for coating
1 tablespoon	**olive oil**

Coarsely chop the ahi and place in a large bowl. Add the rest of the ingredients except the panko flakes and oil. Lightly mix the ingredients in the bowl. Shape mixture into balls (about the size of a large walnut) and roll in panko flakes. Chill for at least two hours. Make the broth below . . .

For Broth		
⅓ cup	**celery,** finely diced
⅓ cup	**carrots,** finely diced
⅓ cup	**Maui onion,** finely diced
¼ cup	**olive oil**
	salt and **pepper,** to taste
2	**bay leaves**
6	sliced fresh **garlic cloves**
½ teaspoon	**marjoram**
1 teaspoon	**fennel seeds**
2 cups	**dry white wine**
2 cups	**chicken or vegetable broth**
1 can (28 ounces)	**whole pear tomatoes**
1 cup	**clam juice**
⅛ cup	**lemon juice**

In a heavy pot, saute celery, carrots and onion in olive oil for ten minutes over medium heat until translucent. Season with salt and pepper. (Be careful not to over-salt.) Add bay leaves, sliced garlic cloves, marjoram and fennel seeds. Cook for one more minute.

Add white wine and broth. Bring to boil for five minutes then add tomatoes. Continue cooking for 45 minutes. Add clam juice and lemon juice. Cook for 10 more minutes.

While broth is simmering, sauté the Ahi balls in a non-stick pan with a small amount of olive oil. Sauté until golden brown on all sides. Remove to a plate lined with a paper towel.

To serve: Warm the soup bowls in a low oven or the dishwasher! Place two of the cooked Ahi balls in each of the bowls. Ladel a cup of soup over them. Garnish with some freshly sautéed corn kernels and fresh chopped cilantro. Finish with a drizzle of sour cream over the soup. Serve immediately.

Serves 4

HAWAIIAN STYLE DESSERTS AND DRINKS

After a full day at the beach, the waves can start
to look like whipped cream. The sand is as hot as puff pastry
straight out of the oven, and the setting sun
is the color of strawberry papaya . . .

Hey, that's when you know it's time to go home,
cool off with an island style drink and make some dessert!

HAWAIIAN STYLE DESSERTS, DRINKS AND SMOOTHIES

KEIKI DRINKS

Keiki, of course, means child in Hawaiian.
Maui Tacos was asked to do the catering in Los Angeles for the
Lilo and Stitch movie premier. While serving up these kid-friendly
drinks, we met lots of folks who loved Hawaii and the movie's
Hawaiian themes just as much as we do.
So, here's a sweet little taste of Aloha . . . for all ages.

CARAMEL MIRANDA

It's time to PARTY!!! This explosion of taste and color
is Chef Mark's signature dessert. Serve it on one big platter and
let guests spoon their portions into individual bowls. Still too formal?
Just have everyone "go for it" straight from the serving platter with
long-handled iced tea spoons!

Mark likes to include a "novelty" food item in his party dishes
to get folks talking. In this recipe it's baby coconuts.
Look for these tiny coconuts in the produce specialty section.
They are no bigger than large marbles and can be eaten whole.

Caramel	2 cups	**sugar**
Sauce:	1/2 cups	**water**
	1/4 teaspoon	**cream of tartar**
	1 cup	**heavy cream**
	1/4 pound	**unsalted butter**
Suggested Fruits	1 cup	diced fresh Hawaiian **pineapple**
to include on	1 cup	diced fresh **mango**
the platter:	1 cup	diced **strawberry papaya**
	1 cup	**baby coconuts** (or shaved coconut)
	1 cup	fresh **raspberries**
	1 cup	fresh **blackberries**
	1 cup	**banana,** sliced on diagonal
	1/2 cup	**dark chocolate** pistols, Hawaiian if possible
	1/2 cup	**white chocolate,** Hawaiian if possible
	4 cups	**macadamia nut ice cream**
		fresh **mint sprigs**
	1/2 cup	diced **macadamia nuts,** roasted and unsalted

In heavy sauté pan, whisk together the sugar, water and cream of tartar over high heat. Stir constantly until it is golden brown. Remove from heat and and whisk in the cream. Whisk in the butter. Keep the caramel sauce warm, but not hot.

Drizzle the caramel sauce on a large oven-proof plate or platter. Arrange the prepared fruit and chocolate on top. Carefully put plate in a pre-heated 350 degree oven. Heat until hot and the chocolate is melting.

Scoop the ice cream right on the middle of the platter immediately before serving. Garnish the plate with fresh mint and sprinkle roasted diced macadamia nuts over it all.

Note: If you prefer individual servings, scoop a portion of ice cream, fruit and sauce on each serving plate. Garnish and serve immediately with a great Hawaiian coffee and raw sugar.

Serves 4 generously!!!

BIG ISLAND CHOCOLATE TORTE SOUFFLÉ

*Did you know they grow outrageously good chocolate
on the Big Island of Hawaii? Try using some in this elegant chocolate dessert.
It really isn't that hard to make if you have a good mixer.
(Didn't everyone on the planet get one for either a Christmas or a wedding gift?)*

⅛ cup	**flour**
¼ pound	unsalted **butter** (+ 2 tablespoons to grease pan)
½ pound	**bittersweet chocolate**
1 cup	**ricotta cheese**
5	**eggs,** separated
2	**egg whites**
⅓ cup	**sugar**
½ teaspoon	**cream of tartar**

Garnish for finished cake:

2 cups	chilled fresh **whipped cream**
1 cup	grated **bittersweet chocolate**

Generously coat the inside of a 10″ round by 2″ deep cake pan with a tablespoon of soft unsalted butter. Sprinkle the buttered pan with flour, shake pan to remove excess flour. Place pan in freezer for 30 minutes. Then repeat process.

Melt ¼ pound of butter and bittersweet chocolate in double boiler. Stir until chocolate and butter are very smooth. Remove from heat and set aside.

Put all of the ricotta, 5 egg yolks and ¼ cup sugar in a large bowl. Beat for three to five minutes until smooth and creamy.

In a separate large bowl, whip the seven (7) egg whites and cream of tartar to a soft peaks stage. Add remaining sugar. Whip until stiff peaks form.

Thoroughly incorporate the chocolate mixture with the ricotta mixture.

Add one large spoonful of the whipped egg whites into the chocolate-ricotta mix and stir well. Then gently fold entire chocolate-ricotta mixture back into the whipped egg whites, being careful not to over mix.

Remove prepared pan from freezer and shake off excess flour. Pour chocolate ricotta mixture into pan.

Bake at 300 degrees for one hour and ten minutes. Cool torte to room temperature. Invert onto a plate.

Frost cake with chilled whipped cream and sprinkle with the grated chocolate. Cool cake for fifteen minutes in the refrigerator before serving.

Makes one cake

MAUI TACOS TROPICAL FRUIT SALSA

This is an incredibly versatile salsa. Great over a rich macadamia nut ice cream,
Mark also likes to serve this fruity mix— instead of syrup—
with French toast, waffles or pancakes. "Try it spooned over yogurt. Ono . . ."

This is best if prepared just before serving, but it can be made ahead of time.
The local fruit varieties may be hard to find. No worries.
The important thing is to use fresh ingredients at their peak of flavor.

¼ cup	**apple banana**
¼ cup	**pineapple,** low acid Hawaiian Gold preferred
¼ cup	Hana wild **rose apple** (or any tart apple)
¼ cup	fresh or canned **lychees**
¼ cup	**strawberries**
¼ cup	**strawberry papaya**
2 teaspoon	fresh **mint,** julienne
2 teaspoon	**lime juice,** fresh squeezed
2 teaspoon	**rose water** (in gourmet or health food stores)

Dice all fruit (¼″ cubes) and gently toss together in a glass, ceramic or other non-reactive bowl with the mint, lime juice and rose water. Keep covered and refrigerated until ready to serve.

Serve over ice cream or pound cake. This salsa is also great served in a decorative bowl at the breakfast table. Simply spoon it over pancakes, waffles or individual servings of French toast.

Makes 1½ cups

SWEET TORTILLA TRIANGLES

Dessert anyone? Flour tortillas to the rescue.
These light wedges, sprinkled with cinnamon sugar are so simple.
Serve them for dessert . . . alone or with a coffee flavored ice cream.

4   **flour tortillas**
    vegetable oil for frying
    cinnamon and **granulated sugar** to taste

Heat the oil to 350 degrees in a heavy skillet.

Meanwhile, stack the tortillas and cut through the stack so the tortillas will be cut exactly in half. Continue cutting the stacks in half until they are cut into wedges the size you prefer.

Gently slide some of the wedges into the hot oil from a spatula. Cook only a few at a time to prevent crowding. Remove wedges from the oil when they are lightly browned and crisp. Repeat. Drain fried wedges on paper towels.

While still warm, sprinkle with cinnamon and sugar to taste.

Serve with fresh sliced fruit and a bowl of whipped cream, Mac Nut ice cream, or even a low calorie fruit salsa.

Serves 4

PLANTATION STYLE
ICED TEA

A tall glass of this tea will make you forget the temperature is soaring.
A plain and inexpensive tea actually works best for this drink.

8	**tea bags**
4 cups	**boiling water**
¼ cup	**sugar** (optional)
¼ cup	**pineapple juice**
4 cups	**crushed ice**
	mint sprigs

Steep the tea bags in the boiling water in a heat resistant glass container or pitcher for about 10 minutes. Remove the tea bags. Stir in the sugar to taste, if desired. Let tea cool to room temperature.

Pour the pineapple juice into the tea and stir. Pour over crushed ice in tall glasses with a sprig of mint.

Makes 4 servings

BASIC SMOOTHIE

*We love smoothies . . . so quick and healthy. Some people slam them down,
but we savor them. They taste great, smell heavenly, look divine and
feel so cool on a hot day.*

2 cups	**fruit,** any kind, peeled and chopped
¼ cup	**ice**
¼ cup	**plain yogurt**

Process all of the ingredients in a blender on high until smooth. Pour into a tall glass.

Makes a single large drink

KONA MOCHA ME
SMOOTHIE FOR TWO

The coffee is for the adult in you . . . the Ovaltine brings out the kid.

2 cups	brewed **coffee**
½ cup	**milk**
1	**banana,** sliced
¼ cup	**orange juice**
4 tablespoons	**Ovaltine** or chocolate mix
2 cups	**crushed ice**

Blend on high in a blender until frothy. Pour into tall glasses. Can be served with whipped cream topped with a chocolate covered coffee bean!

Makes two large drinks

MARK'S FAVORITE SMOOTHIE

Drink your fruit! This is so healthy—low in calories and fat, high on energy, fiber and vitamins.

1	**papaya,** peeled and seeded
1	**apple,** peeled and seeded
1	**apple banana,** sliced
4	**strawberries** stemmed
¼ cup	**crushed ice**
¼ cup	plain **yogurt**
2 tablespoons	**wheat germ** or ground **flax seed**
1 squirt	**orange flower water**

Blend and serve in a frozen glass with a straw. Garnish with a pineapple spear and a sprig of mint.

Makes a single large drink

PINEAPPLE BANANA CINNAMON SMOOTHIE

A delicious breakfast smoothie everyone will enjoy.

1 cup	sliced **banana**
1 cup	Hawaiian **pineapple** (fresh or canned)
2 teaspoons	**brown sugar**
1 teaspoon	ground **cinnamon**
2 cups	**coconut milk** (or regular milk)

Put all ingredients into a blender. Blend for 15 to 30 seconds and serve

4 servings

DIAMOND HEAD
LAVA FLOW

This is a colorful variation on a tropical smoothie.
The syrup oozes down the slushy drink like lava.

2	sliced **bananas**
1 cup	**pineapple juice**
1 cup	**milk**
8	**ice cubes**
	strawberry or **blue vanilla syrup** (optional)

Process the banana, pineapple juice, milk and ice cubes in a blender for 30 seconds.
Pour into four clear tall glasses. Top with 1 ounce of Strawberry or Blue Vanilla
syrup over each serving.

Serve with straws and palm tree stir sticks.

4 servings

LILO'S HILO PUNCH

Anyone from Hanapepe to Hilo can tell you this is a much-loved
drink in the islands. Mark says it makes great Popsicles, too.

2 cups	**orange juice**
2 cups	**guava nectar**
2 cups	**passion fruit juice** (or nectar)
2 tablespoons	**shredded coconut**

Mix the juices together and chill in a glass pitcher or container in the refrigerator.
Pour juice over a glass of ice. Garnish with shredded coconut on top and a colored
straw.

4 servings

TUTU'S STRAWBERRY PINEAPPLE ICE TEA

The decorative and tasty pineapple spears can be
made ahead and kept in the refrigerator.

4	**pineapple spears,** fresh or canned (4″ long)
2 teaspoons	**strawberry syrup**
4 cups	**iced tea** (use 6 teabags in 4 cups of water)
4 cups	**crushed ice**

Place pineapple spears in a bowl. Drizzle strawberry syrup on the pineapple and let them sit for 15 minutes.

Meanwhile, make the tea. Strain tea over the crushed ice in a tall glass. Garnish with a pineapple spear and a tropical umbrella.

4 servings

OHANA FRUIT ON THE BOTTOM SHAVE ICE

Here is a family fun drink and dessert rolled into one. It's great for parties . . .
especially in the hot summer months. Mark makes one giant presentation and has
everyone serve themselves by ladling portions into individual glasses.

2 cups	**fruit salad,** canned or fresh
1 cup	cherry **flavored syrup**
	(or assortment of syrups)
4 cups	**crushed ice**
1/2 cup	shredded **coconut**

Place fruit salad in the bottom of a salad bowl.

Place finely crushed ice on top of fruit. Mound the ice to resemble a volcano, then drizzle flavored syrup all over the ice. Sprinkle the top with a little shredded coconut. Have everyone serve them selves by scooping their serving into a sundae glass or cup.

4 servings

HOW TO
MAUI-MEX

BURRITO HOW-TO INSTRUCTIONS

SELECTING THE TORTILLA

Corn or Flour? That's just the beginning when it comes to tortillas. Tortillas come in various sizes, flavors and even unusual colors. To complicate things, they are stacked on many different aisles all over the store, too.

First you have to find them. Depending on where you live, tortillas can end up in the Ethnic / Mexican Food, Bread, Refrigerated, Bakery, Frozen Food, or even, Deli section of the market. They often turn up on the coveted end aisles, too. Health food stores may stock whole wheat, fat free, soy-based and/or gluten free tortillas!

Some of our Maui-Mex recipes call for gourmet tortilla "wraps" to add flavor and color. When prompted to experiment . . . go for it. We suggest you try spinach, chile tomato, jalapeno or garlic tortilla "wraps" in any of the Maui Tacos burrito recipes.

For traditional burritos, use 10″ to 12″ flour tortillas. Of course, the fresher the better! The best choice for a "heart healthy" burrito are tortillas made with whole wheat and without lard.

WARMING THE TORTILLAS FOR BURRITOS

The key to a great burrito is a fresh WARM tortilla. These are the best ways to warm a store-bought tortilla . . .

- **Oven:** Wrap up to six fresh tortillas in aluminum foil. Heat at 350 degrees until warm (about 5–10 minutes). Remove from oven and use one at a time. Rewrap the rest in the foil to keep them warm and pliable. *Novice skill level.*

- **Microwave:** Wrap up to four fresh tortillas in a damp paper towel. Heat on medium for 40 seconds . . . or until warmed through. Use immediately. (Reheating will dry them out.) ALSO: Look for tortilla warmers in kitchen accessory stores. These heat the burritos evenly in the microwave and keep them warm. *Novice skill level.*

- **Stove top:** In a non-stick or cast iron frying pan or griddle, warm tortillas individually over medium high heat for 10 seconds on each side. (Don't add any oil.) *Novice skill level.*

- **Right on the burner:** Tortillas can be warmed on an electric burner or flat glass cooktop on low heat.)Lay a sheet of aluminum foil between the tortilla and the burner to keep it from sticking.) Watch the tortillas closely while warming to prevent scorching. *Almost Professional Skill Level.*

- **Over open flame:** This would typically be an outdoor grill. If done correctly, it will give a fantastic "old Mexico" flavor. Use tongs and fireproof kitchen mitts. *Professional Skill Level.*

BURRITO FOLDING INSTRUCTIONS

WARM the tortillas
Then cover them with foil to keep them pliable and warm.
Now, make the burrito as soon as possible. That's the secret!

FILL the tortilla
Mound the various fillings in the center of the tortilla. Spread the fillings so that each
bite will contain a bit of every ingredient.

The round thing is a tortilla ➤

The fillings go in the middle ➤

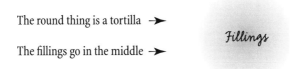

Fillings

FOLD the tortilla
Fold the edges toward the center on the dotted lines as shown. For the last fold,
Mark says: "Fold the tortilla from your stomach." In other words, flip it toward the top
of the plate to finish! The weight of the burrito will hold the tortilla closed.

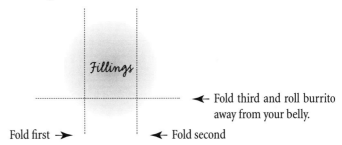

Fillings

◄— Fold third and roll burrito
away from your belly.

Fold first ➤   ◄— Fold second

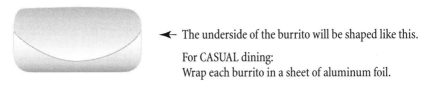

◄— The underside of the burrito will be shaped like this.

For CASUAL dining:
Wrap each burrito in a sheet of aluminum foil.

To serve as an ENTRÉE on a plate:
Place the burrito with the flap facing down.

TACO HOW-TO INSTRUCTIONS

SELECTING THE TORTILLA

Here are the "tortilla rules." Corn or flour tortillas make a great soft shell taco. You need two tortillas for each soft taco. For traditional crunchy style tacos, however, it's best to stick with corn tortillas. Yes, you CAN use flour tortillas for a hard taco if you really want to . . . but they will be greasy. Only one fried tortilla per crunchy taco is needed. In any case, time it so you will use the tortillas prepared any of the following ways *immediately* for the best flavor and texture.

PREPARING THE TORTILLA SHELLS FOR TACOS

Soft Shell Tacos:

- **In a pan.** Use a non-stick or cast iron frying pan or griddle over medium-hot heat. Warm the tortillas individually for 10 seconds per side. When soft, remove from heat and stack in a clean dish towel on a heat resistant plate until ready to use. Heat them just before needed. Don't let them sit for more than a few minutes. *Intermediate skill level.*

- **On the burner:** Warm tortillas on an electric burner of flat glass cooktop. It is best to lay a sheet of aluminum foil between the tortilla and the burner. For the daring, toast the tortillas directly on the burner for a wonderful "nutty" taste. Watch them closely to prevent scorching. *Almost professional level.*

- **In the microwave:** Heat up to four tortillas at a time. Wrap them in a damp paper towel and nuke them on high for less than a minute. Since the moisture content of tortillas varies so much, double check the recommended microwave settings on the tortilla package. *Novice skill level.*

Hard Shell Tacos:

- Use a frying pan that is just slightly larger in diameter than the tortillas you are using. Duh . . . Heat 3/4 of an inch of vegetable oil or shortening in the pan to 350 degrees. Test the temperature by cautiously dipping the edge of a tortilla in the oil. It will sizzle mightily when ready to go . . . and the oil may spit if the tortilla is moist.

- Use tongs to gently slide the corn tortilla into the oil. After the tortilla initially softens, fold the tortilla while it is still in the hot oil. Try to form a half circle . . . but not exactly in half. The top edges of the tortilla should be 1 to 2 inches apart. Keep frying until the tortilla's underside is crispy, then turn the tortilla over with the tongs to fry the other side until equally crispy. Do not let the tortilla turn brown.

- Remove and drain each fried tortilla on a dry paper towel. Let it cool slightly. Set each finished shell in a taco shell holder . . . or hold it in your hand so it is easy to fill. (We hope you have help at this point. While not impossible, it's hard to fry and fill at the same time.)

- Begin frying the next taco shell immediately so the oil doesn't overheat. You may need to add extra oil if you are frying a lot of taco shells.

MAUI TACOS BIOGRAPHIES

MARK ELLMAN,
Maui Tacos Founder / Executive Chef / Owner / Madman

Chef Mark Ellman not only created Maui-Mex cuisine, he is one of the original members of the Hawaii Regional Cuisine movement. His "Pacific Rim" recipes are featured in *"The New Cuisine of Hawaii,"* along with a dozen of his fellow HRC chef friends including Peter Merriman, Roy Yamaguchi, Alan Wong, Beverly Gannon and Sam Choy.

Mark and his wife Judy opened their dream restaurant *Avalon* in Lahaina in the late 1980s. Avalon set the standard for Maui's dining scene for a nearly a decade. In 1993 they opened the first Maui Tacos in Napili and sold Avalon to concentrate on the phenomenal growth of the Maui Tacos chain. In a few short years, Mark, Judy and friend Shep Gordon, had opened seven Maui Tacos on three islands!

"Maui Tacos was created to fill a niche in the beach culture that is Hawaii. It's a place where you can come in with sand on your feet, just to put some good food in your body . . . and get right back to the waves again."

Yes, it's true that celebrities do hang out with the surfers at Maui Tacos. Before they came to Maui, Mark and Judy owned the 'Can't Rock & Roll, But Sure Can Cook' catering company in Los Angeles. They provided catering on film locations and backstage for celebrity rock groups including The Beach Boys, Neil Diamond and the Moody Blues. Check out the autographed photos at the various Maui Tacos locations.

Today Mark personally directs the openings of all the new locations. The Maui Tacos franchise was named one of the top 50 restaurant franchises in the United States for 1999 by Nation's Restaurant News (The NRN Fifty-The New Taste Makers.) There are Maui Tacos in Hawaii and around the Mainland including Georgia, Alabama, New York, New Jersey, Washington D.C., and Minnesota.

Mark is a frequent guest on national (and international) television shows including *Emeril Live, Great Chefs of Hawaii* and the *Today Show*. Mark and Judy live (in that lovely house on the beach) in Lahaina, Maui.

CHEF PEPE VEGA,
Maui Tacos Operations Director

Chef Jose "Pepe" Vega is operations director of Maui Tacos in Hawaii. Pepe found a culinary soulmate in Mark Ellman, who gave him the opportunity to create a Maui-Mex menu full of satisfying Mexican food using traditional techniques and lots of Hawaiian ingredients.

Vega's training began while growing up in his traditional Mexican family. His biggest influence is his mother, also a chef, who taught both Mexican and Spanish cooking classes. His own culinary career was launched in 1985 when he moved from Mexico to Honolulu to work with Chef Alfonso Navarro at the Compadres restaurant chain. He worked his way up from a cook to executive chef and traveled from Honolulu to Australia, San Francisco, Monterey and Napa.

But Pepe missed Hawaii and came back to Maui to work for Ellman in 1995. "I feel very lucky to work for the past few years along the side of one of the best chefs in the world, Mr. Mark Ellman." Mark is just as pleased to have Pepe on the Maui Tacos team, of course. Pepe is also a principal partner in Penne Pasta Café restaurant on Maui.

Pepe believes in using locally grown produce for the added flavor and freshness so important in things like a good salsa fresca. In his mind, creating extraordinary food is simply coupling the best ingredients with a great recipe . . . and he has plenty of those!

EXECUTIVE CHEF SERGIO PEREZ

Chef Sergio Perez was born in Mexico City. According to Mark, "Sergio came into this world destined to cook. He has been around the flavors and smells of kitchens, listening to the ratata-tat of chopping knives of his father's Carnitas Café in the heart of Mexico City." Sergio's father taught him the art of butchering and salsa making, and the importance of pleasing the public.

Sergio's culinary adventures brought him to the Acropolis (a popular Greek restaurant in Lakewood, California!) and then to Maui to work with the new Denny's franchise. Soon Sergio's passion for fine food led him to Avalon Restaurant where he jumped into the world of Pacific Rim cuisine.

Sergio has worked many jobs on Maui (sometimes two at a time) all the while studying at night to become a citizen of the United States. Mark recognized Sergio's talent and named him Executive Chef of Maui Tacos in 1993. Sergio oversees the Hawaii operations and he is a principal partner of Penne Pasta Café in Lahaina.

Sergio is active within the local food scene and travels with the Hawaii Visitors Bureau promoting Hawaii by doing cooking demos. Mark adds, "Sergio's father still runs his taqueria in Mexico some 25 years later. I am sure he is very proud of his son. I know the people of Hawaii are."

BARBARA SANTOS
Food Professional

Barbara writes about food and is best known on Maui for coordinating major food events—including the Maui Onion Festival—for many years. In 1993 she helped create the Maui Writers Conference and the Maui Agricultural Trade Show & Sampling at Tedeschi Vineyards.

Barbara is also the author of ***The Maui Onion Cookbook.*** She and her husband split their time between Maui and Livermore, California. She is currently the marketing director for both the San Francisco Writers Conference and Pendulum Publishing.

INDEX OF RECIPES BY CATEGORY